AAT

Qualifications and Credit Framework (QCF)
LEVEL 3 DIPLOMA IN ACCOUNTING

TEXT

Professional Ethics in
Accounting and
Finance

2010 Edition
(reprinted in 2011)

First edition July 2010

ISBN 9780 7517 8822 8

British Library Cataloguing-in-Publication Data
A catalogue record for this book is available from the British Library

Published by

BPP Learning Media Ltd
BPP House
Aldine Place
London
W12 8AA

www.bpp.com/learningmedia

Printed in the United Kingdom

CONTENTS

INTRODUCTION

This is a time of great change for the AAT. From 1 July 2010 the AAT's assessments will fall within the **Qualifications and Credit Framework** and most papers will be assessed by way of an on demand **computer based assessment**. BPP Learning Media has reacted to this change by investing heavily to produce new ground breaking market leading resources. In particular, our **new suite of online resources** ensures that students are prepared for online testing by means of an online environment where tasks mimic the style of the AAT's assessment tasks.

The BPP range of resources comprises:

- **Texts**, covering all the knowledge and understanding needed by students, with numerous illustrations of 'how it works', practical examples and tasks for students to use to consolidate their learning. The majority of tasks within the texts have been written in an interactive style that reflects the style of the online tasks the AAT will set. Texts are available in our traditional paper format and, in addition, as E-books that can be downloaded to your PC or laptop.

- **Question Banks**, including additional learning questions plus the AAT's practice assessment and a number of other full practice assessments. Full answers to all questions and assessments, prepared by BPP Learning Media, are included. For the first time our question banks are available in an online environment, which mimics the AAT's testing environment. This enables you to familiarise yourself with the environment in which you will be tested.

- **Passcards,** which are handy pocket sized revision tools designed to fit in a handbag or briefcase to enable students to revise anywhere at anytime. All major points are covered in the passcards, which have been designed to assist you in consolidating knowledge.

- **Workbooks,** which have been designed to cover the units that are assessed by way of project/case study. The workbooks contain many practical tasks to assist in the learning process and also a sample assessment or project to work through.

- **Lecturers' resources**, providing a further bank of tasks, answers and full practice assessments for classroom use, available separately only to lecturers whose colleges adopt BPP Learning Media material. The lecturers resources are available in both paper format and online in E-format.

This Text for Professional Ethics in Accounting and Finance has been written specifically to ensure comprehensive yet concise coverage of the AAT's new learning outcomes and assessment criteria. It is fully up to date as at June 2010 and reflects both the AAT's unit guide and the practice assessment provided by the AAT.

Each chapter contains:

- Clear, step by step explanation of the topic

- Logical progression and linking from one chapter to the next

- Numerous illustrations of 'how it works'

- Interactive tasks within the text of the chapter itself, with answers at the back of the book. In general, these tasks have been written in the interactive form that students will see in their real assessments

- Test your learning questions of varying complexity, again with answers supplied at the back of the book. In general these test questions have been written in the interactive form that students will see in their real assessments

The emphasis in all tasks and test questions is on the practical application of the skills acquired.

If you have any comments about this book, please e-mail suedexter@bpp.com or write to Sue Dexter, Publishing Director, BPP Learning Media Ltd, BPP House, Aldine Place, London W12 8AA.

ASSESSMENT STRATEGY

The Professional Ethics in Accounting and Finance (PEAF) assessment is normally a 1.5 hour computer based assessment.

The assessment is split into two sections, consisting of 8 tasks in Section 1 and 10 in Section 2, which will include a broad range of topics across the assessment criteria for this unit.

Competency

Learners will be required to demonstrate competence in both sections of the assessment. For the purpose of assessment the competency level for AAT assessment is set at 70 per cent. The level descriptor in the table below describes the ability and skills students at this level must successfully demonstrate to achieve competence.

QCF Level descriptor	Summary
	Achievement at level 3 reflects the ability to identify and use relevant understanding, methods and skills to complete tasks and address problems that, while well defined, have a measure of complexity. It includes taking responsibility for initiating and completing tasks and procedures as well as exercising autonomy and judgement within limited parameters. It also reflects awareness of different perspectives or approaches within an area of study or work.
	Knowledge and understanding
	■ Use factual, procedural and theoretical understanding to complete tasks and address problems that, while well defined, may be complex and non-routine
	■ Interpret and evaluate relevant information and ideas
	■ Be aware of the nature of the area of study or work
	■ Have awareness of different perspectives or approaches within the area of study or work
	Application and action
	■ Address problems that, while well defined, may be complex and non routine
	■ Identify, select and use appropriate skills, methods and procedures
	■ Use appropriate investigation to inform actions
	■ Review how effective methods and actions have been

	Autonomy and accountability ■ Take responsibility for initiating and completing tasks and procedures, including, where relevant, responsibility for supervising or guiding others ■ Exercise autonomy and judgement within limited parameters

AAT UNIT GUIDE

Professional Ethics in Accounting and Finance (PEAF)

Introduction

This unit guide relates to the Level 3 Unit on Professional Ethics in Accounting and Finance. It should be read in conjunction with the NOS standards and QCF standards for this unit. The aim of this guide is to provide further detail and additional advice for tutors delivering the Professional Ethics in Accounting and Finance unit of the AAT Level 3 Diploma. This guide includes detail on the topics covered within the unit, and the depth and breadth to which these topics need to be taught and learnt.

The purpose of the unit

This knowledge unit recognises the importance of the ethical duties of an accounting technician. Its purpose is to support learners in:

- Working within the AAT's Guidelines on Professional Ethics and other codes

- Promoting public confidence in accountancy practices or functions

- Enhancing the professional reputation and integrity of the learner and their organisation

Learning objectives

In the Professional Ethics in Accounting and Finance unit, learners develop an understanding of the importance of fulfilling the ethical duties that they have as accounting technicians. This involves recognising not only the rules with which they must comply, but also the principles on which these rules are based. Behaving ethically, and knowing when to take action on suspicions or knowledge of unethical behaviour and non- compliance with laws and regulations, protects the professional reputation of accounting technicians, their organisations, the AAT and the accountancy profession as a whole. The result should be the continuing confidence of the public in accountants to protect the public interest. Learners therefore need to know what it means to behave ethically and also what to do if they become aware of any ethical issues in their environment.

Learning outcomes

This unit consists of three learning outcomes:

1. Understand the principles of ethical working in accountancy or payroll.

2. Know how to behave in an ethical manner when working with internal and external customers.

3. Understand when and how to take appropriate action following any suspected breaches of ethical codes.

Delivery guidance

When teaching this unit tutors must stress the relevance and value of all three learning outcomes to all learners. Learners should be encouraged to become very familiar with the AAT Guidelines on Professional Ethics over the course of delivery of the unit, and should be aware of the particular issues referred to in the Guidelines.

QCF Unit	Learning Outcome	Assessment Criteria	Covered in Chapter
Professional Ethics in Accounting and Finance	Understand the principles of ethical working in accountancy or payroll	Explain the principles of ethical behaviour including integrity (including honesty), objectivity, professional and technical competence and due care, confidentiality, professional behaviour	1
		Summarise the relevant legal, regulatory and ethical requirements affecting the accounting and finance sector and your own industry	1
		Explain the role of professional bodies relevant to your work	1
		Explain why you, your organisation or industry are expected to operate within codes of conduct and practice	1
		Explain how organisations can be at risk from improper practice and why it is important to be vigilant	1 & 2
		Identify opportunities to maintain your continuing professional development in line with the requirements of relevant professional bodies	1

QCF Unit	Learning Outcome	Assessment Criteria	Covered in Chapter
	Know how to behave in an ethical manner when working with internal and external customers	Explain how to act appropriately and with integrity, honesty, fairness and sensitivity when working with clients, suppliers, colleagues and others	2
		Identify why it is important to keep a professional distance between professional duties and personal life at all times	2,3
		Explain why it is important to adhere to organisational and professional values, codes of practice and regulations at all times	1
		Explain why it is important to adhere to policies for handling clients' monies	3
		Explain why information should be kept confidential	1 & 3
		Identify circumstances when confidential information should be disclosed and who is entitled to the information	1 & 3
		Explain the importance of working within the limits and confines of your own professional experience, knowledge and expertise	3
		Summarise the advice to clients on the retention of books, working papers and other documents	3

QCF Unit	Learning Outcome	Assessment Criteria	Covered in Chapter
	Understand when and how to take appropriate action following any suspected breaches of ethical codes	Identify the relevant authorities and internal departments to whom unethical behaviour, breaches of confidentiality, suspected illegal acts or other malpractice should be reported	4
		Recognise when the relevant authority should be advised if an employee has concerns over work they have been asked to complete	4
		Identify any inappropriate client behaviour and how to report it to the relevant authority	4
		Explain the procedures which should be followed if an employee suspects an employer, colleague or client has committed, or may commit, an act which is believed to be illegal or unethical eg whistle blowing	1 & 4

Delivery guidance

1. Understand the principles of ethical working in accountancy or payroll

1.1 Explain the principles of ethical behaviour including integrity (including honesty), objectivity, professional and technical competence and due care, confidentiality, professional behaviour

- State the fundamental principles as set out in Part A AAT Guidelines on Professional Ethics ss100 - 150:

    - Integrity
    - Objectivity
    - Professional competence and due care
    - Confidentiality
    - Professional behaviour

- State the types of threat to fundamental principles and safeguards against them as set out in ss100.10 – s100.15 AAT Guidelines on Professional Ethics

- Specify how the conceptual framework of threats and safeguards is designed to operate

- Identify differences between the principles-based approach and a rules-based approach

1.2 <u>Summarise the relevant legal, regulatory and ethical requirements affecting the accounting and finance sector and your own industry</u>

- Identify the importance of compliance with the law (civil and criminal), with other regulations and with guidelines on professional ethics

- State the legal status of the AAT Guidelines on Professional Ethics and their application to members in practice (Part B s 200) and members in business (Part C s 300)

- Identify the limits of the AAT Guidelines, for example that "holding clients' money when running an investment business is subject to detailed FSA rules"

- State the objectives of the accountancy profession (AAT Guidelines on Professional Ethics 1.11)

- Identify in outline the methods by which the accountancy and finance profession is regulated eg in the UK, the role of the FRC and its constituent boards

- Identify other forms of regulation affecting the accountancy and finance sector eg health and safety regulations, environmental regulations

- Identify other methods of regulating industries eg self-regulation, independent watchdogs, ombudsmen, government regulation

- Specify the basics of business ethics (in addition to professional ethics) eg codes of principles and values that govern decisions and actions within an organisation including the impact of the 'tone at the top' on corporate culture

1.3 <u>Explain the role of professional bodies relevant to your work</u>

- Specify the nature and role of, and relationship between, professional bodies that are relevant to their work, including the AAT, the CCAB bodies and IFAC

- Identify the nature and role of industry-related bodies eg the FSA in the UK

1.4 <u>Explain why you, your organisation or industry are expected to operate within codes of conduct and practice</u>

- State the legal status of codes of conduct and codes of practice in general, including industry- or organisation-specific ethical codes

- State the objectives and functions of codes of conduct/codes of practice

- Identify the reasons why individuals, organisations and industries should operate within such codes, including the I DO BEST model

1.5 Explain how organisations can be at risk from improper practice and why it is important to be vigilant

- Identify an appropriate definition of operational risk and factors which give rise to such risk, eg the Basel Committee on Banking Supervision definition

- Specify types of operational risk that arise from improper practice, eg process, people, systems, legal and event risks

- State the rules of customer due diligence (AAT Guidelines on Professional Ethics s210.4)

1.6 Identify opportunities to maintain your continuing professional development in line with the requirements of relevant professional bodies

- Identify their obligations in relation to CPD including the CPD Cycle (AAT Guidelines on Professional Ethics ss1.11, 100.4, 100.12, 130.3 and 200.3, and AAT Guidelines and Regulations for Members in Practice)

2 Know how to behave in an ethical manner when working with internal and external customers

2.1 Explain how to act appropriately and with integrity, honesty, fairness and sensitivity when working with clients, suppliers, colleagues and others

- Identify descriptions of behaviour that demonstrate integrity, honesty, fairness and sensitivity (including Part C AAT Guidelines on Professional Ethics s320)

- Specify circumstances in which ethical behaviour is required (when liaising with clients, suppliers, colleagues and others)

- Identify behaviour that is both ethical and appropriate in a given set of circumstances, and behaviour that is unethical and inappropriate

- Identify how safeguards are used to address threats to the fundamental principles in a given set of circumstances (Part A AAT Guidelines on Professional Ethics ss100-150, Part B AAT Guidelines on Professional Ethics s200, Part C AAT Guidelines on Professional Ethics s300)

- State the relevant AAT Guidelines on Professional Ethics in relation to professional appointment (s210), conflicts of interest (s220), second opinions (s230), fees and other types of remuneration (s240), marketing professional services (s250), agencies (s251), letters of engagement (s252), and names and letterheads of practices (s253)

2.2 Identify why it is important to keep a professional distance between professional duties and personal life at all times

- State what should be done about threats associated with lack of professional distance (including Part B AAT Guidelines on Professional Ethics [conflicts of interest s220] and Part C AAT Guidelines on Professional Ethics [financial interests s340])

- State the appropriate guidance on maintaining objectivity in Part B AAT Guidelines on Professional Ethics s280

- State the appropriate guidance on gifts and hospitality for a member in practice (Part B AAT Guidelines on Professional Ethics s260) and on inducements for a member in business (Part C AAT Guidelines on Professional Ethics s350)

- State the appropriate guidance on maintaining independence in an assurance engagement (Part B AAT Guidelines on Professional Ethics s290)

2.3 Explain why it is important to adhere to organisational and professional values, codes of practice and regulations at all times

- Identify key organisational and professional values (including the Nolan principles)

- Specify the effect of codes of practice and regulations on the individual, and the consequences of non-compliance including disciplinary action (an outline knowledge of the AAT process as set out in the Disciplinary Regulations for Members is required)

2.4 Explain why it is important to adhere to policies for handling clients' monies

- State appropriate policies for handling clients' money (Part B AAT Guidelines on Professional Ethics s 270)

- Specify potential consequences of non-compliance with policies: money laundering, breach of investment business rules, fraud (Fraud Act 2006 offences)

2.5 Explain why information should be kept confidential

- Specify the importance of confidentiality, including both the fundamental principle (Part A AAT Guidelines on Professional Ethics s 140.1-140.6) and legal rules (Data Protection Act 1998 and the role of the Information Commissioner's Office)

2.6 Identify circumstances when confidential information should be disclosed and who is entitled to the information

- Specify the disclosure rules and matters to consider in deciding whether to disclose (Part A AAT Guidelines on Professional Ethics s 140.7-140.8)

- Identify from a given set of circumstances the appropriate course of action regarding disclosure

- Identify in a given set of circumstances the appropriate person/organisation to whom disclosure should be made

2.7 Explain the importance of working within the limits and confines of your own professional experience, knowledge and expertise

- State the importance of working within their professional experience, knowledge and expertise, including an outline of contractual relationships, professional negligence, breach of trust and the Fraud Act 2006

- Identify the broad issues regarding breach of contract by members in practice (Part B AAT Guidelines on Professional ethics s257)

- State the guidance on acting with sufficient expertise for a member in business (Part C AAT Guidelines on Professional Ethics s330)

- Identify the appropriate response to requests for them to work outside the confines of their own professional experience and expertise in a given set of circumstances

2.8 Summarise the advice to clients on the retention of books, working papers and other documents

- State the guidance on ownership of books and records (s254), lien (s255) and retention of books, working papers and other documents (s256) set out in Part B AAT Guidelines on Professional Ethics

3 Understand when and how to take appropriate action following any suspected breaches of ethical codes

3.1 Identify the relevant authorities and internal departments to whom unethical behaviour, breaches of confidentiality, suspected illegal acts or other malpractice should be reported

- Identify the money laundering/terrorist financing offences and their consequences

- Identify the relevant authority to which reports should be made namely:

- Money Laundering Reporting Officer (MLRO) or Serious Organised Crime Agency (SOCA) regarding money laundering

- MLRO/SOCA regarding tax errors/omissions (Part B AAT Guidelines on Professional Ethics s160)

- Other relevant authorities in the UK and elsewhere (eg police re suspected fraud)

- Identify the prescribed internal or external department and/or professional body to which reports should be made regarding breach of codes of conduct/practice or Guidelines

3.2 <u>Recognise when the relevant authority should be advised if an employee has concerns over work they have been asked to complete</u>

- Specify the type of concern that may arise for an employee about work they have been asked to complete (Part C AAT Guidelines on Professional Ethics s 310)

- Identify from a set of circumstances the time at which advice about concerns should be sought from the AAT Ethics Advice Line or employer-run service

3.3 <u>Identify any inappropriate client behaviour and how to report it to the relevant authority</u>

- Specify the type of concern that may arise for a member in practice about inappropriate client behaviour, including the offences of 'tipping off' and failure to disclose

- Identify from a set of circumstances the time at which advice about inappropriate client behaviour should be sought from the AAT Ethics Advice Line

- State how to report inappropriate client behaviour (outline only)

3.4 <u>Explain the procedures which should be followed if an employee suspects an employer, colleague or client has committed, or may commit, an act which is believed to be illegal or unethical eg whistle blowing</u>

- State the rules on members making required disclosures in internal reports and suspicious activities reports regarding money laundering under the Proceeds of Crime Act 2002, and Money Laundering Regulations 2003 and 2007 (AAT Guidelines on Professional Ethics s100.20, 140.7,and s210.5), as set out in Sections 2 and 6 of CCAB's Anti-Money Laundering Guidance for the Accountancy Sector

- Identify the protection available for 'whistle-blowers' under the Public Interest Disclosure Act 1998 (Part C AAT Guidelines on Professional Ethics s330)

chapter 1:
THE PRINCIPLES OF ETHICAL WORKING

chapter coverage 📖

In this opening chapter, we consider the fundamental principles of ethical behaviour as they apply in the general context of the UK accountancy profession, and the framework set out by the AAT's Guidelines on Professional Ethics and the regulatory environment.

We consider the role of the main professional bodies relevant to your work, the importance of codes of conduct and codes of practice in business dealings, and the importance of maintaining your continuing professional development.

The topics we cover are:

✍ What are ethics?

✍ Why behave ethically?

✍ Fundamental ethical principles

✍ The conceptual framework

✍ Principles versus rules

✍ Compliance with the law

✍ The accountancy profession

✍ Codes of conduct and codes of practice

✍ Business ethics and professional values

✍ Risks from improper practice

✍ AAT disciplinary regulations

✍ Continuing professional development (CPD)

WHAT ARE ETHICS?

Ethics are a set of moral principles that guide behaviour.

Ethical values are assumptions and beliefs about what constitutes 'right' and 'wrong' behaviour.

Individuals have ethical values, often reflecting the beliefs of the families, cultures and educational environments in which they developed their ideas.

Organisations also have ethical values, based on the norms and standards of behaviour that their leaders believe will best help them express their identity and achieve their objectives.

The concept of **business ethics** suggests that businesses are morally responsible for their actions, and should be held accountable for the effects of their actions on people and society. This is true for individual businesses (which should behave ethically towards the employees, customers, suppliers and communities who are affected by them) and for 'business' in general, which has a duty to behave responsibly in the interests of the society of which it is a part.

Some of these ethical values may be explicit: included in the organisation's mission statement, set out in ethical codes and guidelines, or taught in employee training programmes. Other values may be part of the **organisation culture**: 'the way we do things around here', the unwritten rules and customs of behaviour that develop over time as people find ways of working together.

A **code of ethics** often focuses on social issues. It may set out general principles about an organisation's beliefs on matters such as mission, quality, privacy or the environment. The effectiveness of such codes of ethics depends on the extent to which management supports them 'from the top'. The code of ethics often gives rise to a **code of conduct** for employees.

Task 1

Think of some examples of the kinds of behaviour that you consider 'right' or 'wrong' in your personal and professional life.

WHY BEHAVE ETHICALLY?

The **AAT Guidelines on Professional Ethics** (on which this text is substantially based) note that: 'the decisions you make in the everyday course of your professional lives can have real ethical implications.'

The AAT Guidelines are in three parts:

- Part A applies to all members

- Part B represents additional guidance which applies specifically to members in practice

- Part C applies specifically to members in business

The **objectives of the accountancy profession** are set out in the AAT Guidelines at paragraph 1.11:

(i) The mastering of **particular skills and techniques** acquired through learning and education and maintained through continuing professional development

(ii) Development of an **ethical approach to work** as well as to employers and clients. This is acquired by experience and professional supervision under training and is safeguarded by strict ethical and disciplinary guidelines

(iii) Acknowledgement of **duties to society** as a whole, in addition to duties to the employer or the client

(iv) An outlook which is essentially **objective**, obtained by being fair minded and free from conflicts of interest

(v) Rendering services to the **highest standards** of conduct and performance

(vi) Achieving **acceptance by the public** that members provide accountancy services in accordance with these high standards and requirements

The AAT Guidelines 'aim to assist members to achieve these objectives'. It suggests several key reasons why an accounting technician should strive to behave ethically:

- Ethical issues may be a matter of **law and regulation**. You are expected to know and apply the **civil and criminal law** of the country in which you live and work – as a basic minimum requirement for good practice. The AAT Guidelines are based on the laws effective in the UK, with which members are expected to comply as a minimum requirement. (It is sometimes said that 'the law is a floor': the lowest acceptable level of behaviour required to preserve the public interest and individual rights.)

- The **AAT** (like other professional bodies) requires its members to conduct themselves, and provide services to clients, according to certain professional and ethical standards. It does this, in part, to maintain its own **reputation and standing** – but this is also of benefit to its members and to the accounting profession as a whole.

- Professional and ethical behaviour protects the **public interest**. The accountancy profession sees itself as having duties to society as a whole – in addition to its specific obligations to employers and clients.

The advice for AAT members, in a nutshell, is as follows:

- Completely avoid even the appearance of **conflict of interest**

- Be **objective** and act in the **public interest,** because your responsibility is not exclusively to satisfy the needs of an individual client or employer

- Keep sensitive information **confidential**. Accountants often deal with their employer's or client's most private material

- Be **straightforward and honest** in professional and business relationships

- Maintain **professional knowledge, behaviour and skills** at the level required by a client or employer

FUNDAMENTAL ETHICAL PRINCIPLES

You MUST print out a copy of the AAT's Guidelines on Professional Ethics from the AAT's website (www.aat.org.uk) and refer to it as you work through the professional ethics unit.

You might have your own ideas about what 'ethical behaviour' looks like – and these ideas will be shaped by your personal assumptions and values, and the values of the culture in which you operate (at work and in the country in which you live). However, there are certain basic or **fundamental principles** set out in the AAT Guidelines that underpin ethical behaviour in an accounting context:

- Integrity
- Objectivity
- Professional competence and due care
- Confidentiality
- Professional behaviour

Let's look at each of these in turn.

Integrity – section 110

"The principle of **integrity** imposes an obligation on all members to be straightforward and honest in professional and business relationships. Integrity also implies fair dealing and truthfulness."(Paragraph 110.1 of the AAT Guidelines).

Paragraph 110.2 goes further:

"A member must not be associated with reports, returns, communications or other information where they believe that the information:

(i) contains a **false or misleading statement**

(ii) contains **statements** or **information furnished recklessly** or

(iii) **omits** or **obscures information** required to be included where such omission or obscurity would be misleading."

On an everyday level, integrity involves matters such as being **open** about the limitations of your knowledge or competence, being **honest** in your relationships and carrying out your work **accurately**, conscientiously and efficiently.

Objectivity – section 120

"The principle of **objectivity** imposes an obligation on all members not to compromise their professional or business judgement because of bias, conflict of interest or the undue influence of others" (Paragraph 120.1).

This is an extremely important principle for the accounting profession because it protects the interests both of the parties directly affected by an accountant's services and of the general public (who rely on the accuracy of information and the integrity of financial systems).

Objectivity is the principle that all professional and business judgements should be made fairly:

- On the basis of an **independent** and intellectually honest appraisal of information

- **Free from** all forms of **prejudice** and **bias**

- Free from factors which might affect **impartiality**, such as pressure from a superior, financial interest in the outcome, a personal or professional relationship with one of the parties involved, or a conflict of interest (where one client stands to lose and another to gain by a particular disclosure)

Task 2

A member who is straightforward and honest in all business and professional relationships can be said to be following the fundamental principle of objectivity.

	✔
True	
False	

Professional competence and due care – section 130

Accountants have an obligation to their employers and clients to know what they are doing – and to do it right! The following is taken from the AAT Guidelines:

130.1 The principle of **professional competence** and due care imposes the following obligations on members:

(i) to maintain **professional knowledge** and **skill** at the level required to ensure that clients or employers receive competent professional service and

(ii) to **act diligently** in accordance with applicable technical and professional standards when providing professional services.

130.2 Competent professional service requires the exercise of **sound judgement** in applying professional knowledge and skill in the performance of such service. Professional competence may be divided into two separate phases:

(i) attainment of professional competence and

(ii) maintenance of professional competence.

130.3 The **maintenance of professional competence** requires continuing awareness and understanding of relevant technical, professional and business developments. Continuing professional development develops and maintains the capabilities that enable a member to perform competently within the professional environment. To achieve this, Council has recommended a programme of relevant CPD which is output based. This requires members to assess, plan, action and evaluate their learning and development needs.

130.4 **Diligence** encompasses the **responsibility** to act in accordance with the requirements of an assignment, carefully, thoroughly and on a timely basis.

130.5 A member should take steps to ensure that those working under the member's authority in a **professional capacity** have appropriate **training** and **supervision**.

130.6 Where appropriate, a member should make clients, employers or other users of the professional services aware of **limitations** inherent in the services to avoid the misinterpretation of an expression of opinion as an assertion of fact.

You should understand from this that you must not agree to carry out a task or assignment if you do not have the competence to carry it out to a **satisfactory standard** – unless you are sure that you will be able to get the help and advice you need to do so. And if you discover in the course of performing a task or assignment that you lack the knowledge or competence to complete it satisfactorily, you should not continue without taking steps to get the help you need.

In addition, once you have become a member of the profession, you need to maintain and develop your professional and **technical competence**, to keep pace with the demands which may be made on you in your work – and developments which may affect your work over time. This may mean:

- Regularly reviewing your practices against national and international standards, codes, regulations and legislation. Are you complying with the latest requirements?

- Continually upgrading your knowledge and skills in line with developments in accounting practices, requirements and techniques – and making sure that you do not get 'rusty' in the skills you have!

Task 3

Identify which of the words in bold is more appropriate in the following sentence:

'Continuing professional development (CPD) is important to accountancy professionals as it helps them **attain/maintain** competency in their role.'

Due care is a legal concept that means that, having agreed to do a task or assignment, you have an obligation to carry it out to the best of your ability, in the client's or employer's best interests, within reasonable timescales and with proper regard for the technical and professional standards expected of you as a professional.

As the expert in your field, you may often deal with others who have little knowledge of accounting matters. This puts you in a position of power, which must never be abused by carrying out your task or assignment in a negligent or 'careless' way.

Confidentiality – section 140

The following is taken from the AAT Guidelines s.140:

"In general terms, there is a legal obligation to maintain the **confidentiality** of information which is given or obtained in circumstances giving rise to a duty of confidentiality. There are some situations where the law allows a breach of this duty.

The following guidelines help to explain what this means in practice for members as well as giving guidance on the standards required of members from an ethical perspective.

140.1 The principle of **confidentiality** imposes an obligation on members to refrain from:

(i)   **disclosing** outside the firm or employing organisation confidential information acquired as a result of professional and business relationships without proper and specific authority or unless there is a legal or professional right or duty to disclose and

(ii) **using confidential information** acquired as a result of professional and business relationships to their personal advantage or the advantage of third parties.

Information about a past, present, or prospective client's or **employer's affairs**, or the affairs of clients of employers, acquired in a work context, is likely to be confidential if it is not a matter of public knowledge.

140.2 A member must take care to maintain confidentiality even in a **social environment.** The member should be alert to the possibility of inadvertent disclosure, particularly in circumstances involving close or personal relations, associates and long established business relationships.

140.3 A member must also maintain confidentiality of information disclosed by a **prospective client** or **employer**.

140.4 A member must also consider the need to maintain confidentiality of information within the firm or **employing organisation**.

140.5 A member must take all **reasonable steps** to ensure that **staff under their control** and persons from whom advice and assistance is obtained **respect** the principle of **confidentiality**. The restriction on using confidential information also means not using it for any purpose other than that for which it was legitimately acquired.

140.6 The need to comply with the principle of confidentiality **continues even after the end of relationships** between a member and a client or employer. When a member changes employment or acquires a new client, the member is entitled to use prior experience. The member must not, however, use or disclose any confidential information either acquired or received as a result of a professional or business relationship.

140.7 The following are **circumstances where members are or may be required to disclose confidential information** or when such disclosure may be appropriate:

(a)   where disclosure is **permitted by law** and is authorised by the client or the employer (or any other person to whom an obligation of confidence is owed)

(b)   where disclosure is **required by law**, for example:

(i)   production of documents or other provision of evidence in the course of **legal proceedings** or

(ii) disclosure to the appropriate **public authorities** (for example, HMRC) of infringements of the law that come to light or

(iii) disclosure of actual or suspected **money laundering** or **terrorist financing** to the member's firm's MLRO or to SOCA if the member is a sole practitioner,

Or

(c) where there is a **professional duty or right to disclose**, which is in the public interest, and is not prohibited by law. Examples may include:

(i) to **comply with the quality review** of an IFAC member body or other relevant professional body

(ii) to **respond to an inquiry or investigation** by the AAT or a relevant regulatory or professional body

(iii) where it is necessary to **protect the member's professional interests** in legal proceedings or

(iv) to **comply with technical standards** and **ethics requirements**.

This is a difficult and complex area and members are therefore specifically advised to **seek professional advice** before disclosing confidential information under c above.

140.8 In deciding whether to disclose confidential information, members should consider the following points:

(i) whether the **interests of all parties**, including third parties, could be harmed even though the client or employer (or other person to whom there is a duty of confidentiality) consents to the disclosure of information by the member

(ii) whether **all the relevant information is known** and substantiated, to the extent that this is practicable. When the situation involves unsubstantiated facts, incomplete information or unsubstantiated conclusions, professional judgement should be used in determining the type of disclosure to be made, if any

(iii) the **type of communication** or disclosure that may be made and by whom it is to be received; in particular, members should be satisfied that the parties to whom the communication is addressed are appropriate recipients.

Members who are in any doubt about their obligations in a particular situation should seek professional advice."

It is important to appreciate that **confidentiality** is an important value in many relationships, both personal and legal. You need to respect the confidentiality of information acquired as a result of professional and business relationships. This means that you will not use or disclose confidential information to others, unless:

- You have **specific** and **'proper' authorisation** to do so by the client or employer

- You are legally or professionally **entitled** or *obliged* to do so

It is also worth being aware that personal information shared with you by clients and colleagues at work should be regarded as confidential – unless you are told otherwise: this is an important basis for trust in any working relationship.

Task 4

In which of the following circumstances do you have a duty to disclose confidential information concerning a customer of your organisation?

	✓
If they are asked for during legal proceedings.	
When your manager tells you to disclose the information.	
When writing a report for general circulation within your organisation.	

Professional behaviour – section 150

The final fundamental principle is professional behaviour. On this principle the AAT Guidelines state:

150.1 The principle of **professional behaviour** imposes an obligation on members to comply with relevant laws and regulations and avoid any action that may bring disrepute to the profession. This includes actions which a reasonable and informed third party, having knowledge of all relevant information, would conclude negatively affect the good reputation of the profession.

Members should note that conduct reflecting adversely on the reputation of the AAT is a ground for disciplinary action under the AAT's Disciplinary Regulations.

150.2 An example of this principle is that in **marketing** and promoting themselves and their work, members must be honest and truthful. They may bring the profession into disrepute if they:

(i) make **exaggerated claims** for the services they are able to offer, the qualifications they possess, or experience they have gained or

(ii) make **disparaging references** or **unsubstantiated comparisons** to the work of others.

Applying this principle means **'being professional'**. You'll have your own ideas about what 'being professional' means, but in a sense, it involves behaving in a way that maintains or enhances the reputation of your profession: bringing it credit – not discredit.

One key aspect of this is **courtesy**. As a professional, you should behave with courtesy and consideration towards anyone with whom you come into contact in the course of your work and indeed in your personal life.

> It is IMPOSSIBLE for us to overstate the importance of each of these fundamental principles – you MUST be able to recognise each of them.

HOW IT WORKS

Now that we've considered the fundamental principles in general, let's consider some typical scenarios in which they might be helpful. In each case, we will identify the ethical issues they present, in line with the basic principles discussed so far. For the purposes of these questions you should assume you are an AAT student.

Incident one

You are asked to produce an aged debtors (receivables) listing for your manager as soon as possible. However you do not have up to date figures because of a problem with the computer system. A colleague suggests that to get the report done in time you use averages for the missing figures.

There is an **integrity** issue here. Using averages instead of actual figures will almost certainly result in an inaccurate listing. You should report the problem to your manager and ask for an extension to your deadline in order to provide an accurate listing.

Incident two

You have received a letter from an estate agent, requesting financial information about one of your company's customers that is applying to rent a property. The information is needed as soon as possible, by fax or e-mail, in order to secure approval for the rent agreement.

There is a **confidentiality** issue here. You need the customer's authority to disclose the information; you may also need to confirm the identity of the person making the request. You should also take steps to protect the confidentiality of the information when you send it: for example, not using fax or e-mail (which can be intercepted), and stating clearly that the information is confidential.

Incident three

While out to lunch, you run into a friend at the sandwich bar. In conversation, she tells you that she expects to inherit from a recently deceased uncle, and asks you how she will be affected by inheritance tax, capital gains tax and other matters.

There are issues of **due care** and **competence** here. You are not qualified to give advice on matters of taxation. Even if you were qualified, any answer you give on the spot would risk being incomplete or inaccurate with potentially serious consequences.

A client of the accountancy practice you work in is so pleased with the service you gave him this year that he offers you a free weekend break in a luxury hotel, just as a 'thank you'.

There is an **objectivity** issue here as the gift is of significant value. Think about how it looks: a third party observer is entitled to wonder what 'special favours' deserve this extra reward – and/or how such a gift may bias you in the client's favour in future.

 Signpost

See the AAT Guidelines on Professional Ethics:

- **Section 100**: Fundamental principles
- **Section 110**: Integrity
- **Section 120**: Objectivity
- **Section 130**: Professional competence and due care
- **Section 140**: Confidentiality
- **Section 150**: Professional behaviour

THE CONCEPTUAL FRAMEWORK

It is impossible to give guidelines on every possible situation that may arise in the course of your work which conflicts with the fundamental ethical principles. The AAT Guidelines therefore set out a basic **problem solving procedure,** which you can use in any situation, to give yourself the best chance of complying with the principles. This procedure forms the '**conceptual framework**' which consists of **threats** and **safeguards**:

- Identify where there may be a **threat** to a fundamental principle

- **Evaluate the threat**: how serious is it?

- For any serious threat **apply safeguards** that will eliminate the threat or reduce it to an acceptable level (so that compliance with the fundamental principle is not compromised)

- If safeguards cannot be applied, **decline or discontinue** the specific action or professional service involved, or where necessary, **resign** from the client (if you are a member in practice) or the employing organisation (if you are a member in business)

The following is an extract from the AAT Guidelines:

100.5 The circumstances in which members operate may give rise to specific threats to compliance with the fundamental principles. It is impossible to define every situation that creates such threats and specify the appropriate mitigating action. In addition, the nature of engagements and work assignments may differ and consequently different threats may exist, requiring the application of different safeguards. A conceptual framework that requires a member to identify, evaluate and address threats to compliance with the fundamental principles, rather than merely comply with a set of specific rules which may be arbitrary, is, therefore, in the public interest.

This **conceptual framework** approach requires members to identify, evaluate and respond to threats to compliance with the fundamental principles. It also requires that if identified threats are not clearly insignificant, a member must, where appropriate, apply adequate safeguards to eliminate the threats or reduce them to an acceptable level, so that compliance with the fundamental principles is not compromised.

100.6 A member has an obligation to **evaluate any threats** to compliance with the fundamental principles when the member knows, or could reasonably be expected to know, of circumstances or relationships that may compromise compliance with the fundamental principles.

100.7 A member should take **qualitative** as well as **quantitative factors** into account when considering the significance of a threat. If a member cannot implement appropriate safeguards, the member should decline or discontinue the specific professional service involved, or where necessary resign from the client (in the case of a member in practice) or the employing organisation (in the case of a member in business).

According to the AAT Guidelines the safeguards against the threats posed to the fundamental principles include:

100.12 **Safeguards** created by the profession, legislation or regulation include, but are not restricted to:

(i)   **educational, training** and **experience** requirements for entry into the profession

(ii)   **continuing professional development** requirements

(iii) **corporate governance** regulations

(iv) **professional standards**

(v)   **professional** or **regulatory monitoring** and **disciplinary procedures**

(vi) **external review** of the reports, returns, communications or information produced by a member and carried out by a legally empowered third party.

We shall now look at what threats and safeguards are in more detail.

Threats

Many of the threats that may create a risk of compromising on the fundamental principles will fall into one of the following categories (section 100.10 of the AAT Guidelines):

- **Self-interest threats**. These occur as a result of financial or other interests of a member or personal relation of a member, for example where you stand to gain a cash bonus for doing (or not doing) something.

- **Self-review threats**. These occur where a previous judgement needs to be re-evaluated by the member responsible for that judgement. For example you are asked to prepare a report when you were involved in preparing the underlying accounting records. The risk is that you will be biased (whether knowingly or not) in your own favour – and there will be no genuine objective check on the work or decision.

- **Familiarity threats**. These occur because of a close or personal relationship and the member becoming sympathetic to the interests of others. For example you may be asked to advise a client with whom you have a family connection, or evaluate the work of a colleague who is also a close friend.

- **Intimidation threats**. These occur where a member becomes deterred from acting objectively by actual or perceived threats. For example, you feel you will lose your job if you do not report favourably on your employer.

- **Advocacy threats**. These occur where a member promotes a position or opinion to the point that subsequent objectivity might be compromised. The risk is that since you have strongly promoted that position or opinion, people will have difficulty in believing that you are objective about the matter or the party you have supported. For example, you might stand up for a supplier that is continuously late in paying their debts, giving the impression that you are 'on their side'.

Safeguards

There are two broad categories of safeguards that you might use to reduce or eliminate threats (section 100.11 and 100.12 of the AAT Guidelines):

- **Safeguards created by the profession and/or legislation and regulation**. Legal rules and professional codes are specifically designed to support ethical behaviour: a partial solution is therefore to comply with the rules! Potential safeguards include:

    - Education and training, as a requirement for entry into the profession

- Continuing professional development whilst within the profession. (Both of these are safeguards because they help you make the right decisions.)

- Corporate governance regulations (eg on internal company controls and financial reporting)

- Professional standards, related monitoring and disciplinary procedures (including complaints procedures and a duty to report breaches of ethical requirements to deter unethical behaviour)

- Third-party review of financial reports and returns produced by members (eg the auditing of accounts)

- **Safeguards in the work environment**, which increase the likelihood of identifying or deterring unethical behaviour, include:

  - Quality controls, and internal audits of quality controls

  - Mechanisms to empower and protect staff who raise ethical concerns ('whistleblowers')

  - Involvement of, or consultation with, independent third parties (eg non executive directors or regulatory bodies)

  - Rotation of personnel to avoid increasing familiarity and opportunities for collusion in fraud

  - Opportunities to discuss ethical dilemmas (eg with an ethics officer, committee or forum)

Specific safeguards are considered in more detail in Chapter 2 in terms of members in practice and members in business.

Task 5

Jake has been put under significant pressure by his manager to change the conclusion of a report he has written which reflects badly on the manager's performance.

Which threat is Jake facing?

	✓
Self-interest	
Advocacy	
Intimidation	

Signpost

See the AAT Guidelines on Professional Ethics:
- Section 100: Conceptual framework approach
- Section 100: Threats and safeguards

PRINCIPLES VERSUS RULES

The AAT could have a taken a **rules-based approach** to ethics. This would have involved creating a large book of rules trying to cover every possible ethical scenario that could be faced, with an answer to every single ethical problem. Instead, its code of ethics is based on fundamental principles, which you should apply in all your work. Codes in the US, such as the Sarbanes-Oxley rules on corporate governance, are often rules-based.

This **principles-based approach** to ethics encourages a case-by-case deliberation, judgement and responsibility that can be applied to the infinite variety of circumstances that arise in the modern business environment. Hopefully, this will encourage a more flexible approach to ethical problems, while at the same time promoting ethical awareness. This approach is advocated by the ethical code of the International Federation of Accountants (IFAC) on which the AAT bases its ethical code.

Consider the pros and cons of the principles- and rules-based approaches:

Rules-based approach – advantages

- Rules are clear-cut, leaving no room for misunderstanding
- The correct course of action is likely to be obvious
- Rules-based approaches are easier to enforce

Rules-based approach – disadvantages

- You can wriggle out of your obligations by finding loopholes; it is often said that rules encourage avoidance

- Promotes a "tick box" mentality, with concern for the letter of the rule, rather than its spirit

- Must legislate for every circumstance, necessitating a large number of detailed requirements

- New requirements must be developed as circumstances change

- Risk of getting swamped by the details and missing the big picture

Principles-based approach – advantages

- Sets more rigorous standards of behaviour as you must comply with the spirit, not just the letter, of the requirements. It is often said that principles encourage compliance
- Helps you see the bigger picture rather than just individual rules
- Flexible – can keep up with a rapidly changing business environment and be applied in differing circumstances across the world
- Promotes the development of ethical judgement and decision-making skills
- Helps create a culture of ethical awareness
- Encourages you to take responsibility for your actions

Principles-based approach – disadvantages

- It is not always easy to find the right answer or even to identify the right questions
- There may be more than one correct course of action and conflicting interests and priorities must be carefully balanced

COMPLIANCE WITH THE LAW

In the UK, law falls into two categories:

- **Criminal law** – offences relating to persons or property that affect the whole community. Criminal punishment for breach of criminal law (for money laundering or fraud, for example) is most likely to result in fines or imprisonment imposed by the state.

- **Civil law** – wrongs relating to conflicts between individuals within the community. A lawsuit for breach of contract, for example, is a civil action and the remedies awarded are designed to place the injured party in the position they would be in were it not for the breach. The concept of punishment does not apply.

Accountants are affected by a range of laws which they should be aware of. Some of them are not necessarily obvious such as **health and safety legislation, environmental regulations** and **employment protection law**.

- Members who are employees have duties under health and safety legislation to take precautions against risk of injury and to report potential risks to management. Members who are self employed have duties to protect the health and safety of their employees.

- All employees have a general duty to behave in ways that contribute to, and maintain, a healthy and safe workplace. Reckless behaviour endangers both yourself and others: creating the risk of accidents, fire, security breach and so on.

- Employment protection law concerns rules on whether an employer can dismiss employees without being liable for claims for wrongful and unfair dismissal. It also includes legislation on treating employees fairly, for example without discriminating against them due to their age, sex, religion or sexual orientation.

When deciding whether or not behaviour is ethical, compliance with the law is assumed as a starting point: "the law is a floor". Section 1.7 of the AAT Guidelines states that:

"The Guidelines are based on the laws effective in the UK **which members are expected to comply with as a minimum requirement**. Members working or living overseas are expected to know and apply the laws of the overseas country, having taken local legal advice if necessary. Where these Guidelines refer to legal issues, they do not purport to give definitive legal advice or to cover every situation, nor do these Guidelines highlight every legal issue that members may need to consider. Members who encounter problems in relation to legal aspects are recommended to seek their own legal advice."

The key point to remember about the AAT's Guidelines is that they are **not legally enforceable**. They are guidelines set by the profession and failing to meet them will **not** result in a member breaking the civil or criminal law. Any penalties are at the discretion of the AAT and subject to the member's conduct adversely reflecting on the reputation of the AAT.

The AAT's guidelines do have **limits** as members are also subject to legal or other regulations depending on the work they do. For example members who are involved in investment business must meet the Financial Services Authority's (FSA) rules on holding clients' money.

THE ACCOUNTANCY PROFESSION

According to the introduction to the AAT's Guidelines (s 1.11) the objectives of the accountancy profession are:

- The mastering of particular skills and techniques acquired through learning and education and maintained through continuing professional development

- Development of an ethical approach to work as well as to employers and clients. This is acquired by experience and professional supervision under training and is safeguarded by strict ethical and disciplinary guidelines

- Acknowledgement of duties to society as a whole in addition to duties to the employer or the client

- An outlook which is essentially objective, obtained by being fair minded and free from conflicts of interest

- Rendering services to the highest standards of conduct and performance

- Achieving acceptance by the public that members provide accountancy services in accordance with these high standards and requirements.

In the UK, the accountancy profession is largely self-regulatory, with the professional accountancy bodies each responsible for setting and upholding the ethical standards of their members. The bodies themselves are under the supervision of the Professional Oversight Board (POB), which is part of the Financial Reporting Council (FRC). It should be noted, however, that the AAT itself is not supervised by the FRC or POB.

The Financial Reporting Council (FRC)

The FRC is the unified, independent regulator for the accountancy and actuarial professions. It was established to promote ethical financial reporting and increased confidence in the accountancy profession, corporate reporting and governance in the UK, through:

- the setting of accounting standards which guide how companies' financial statements should be prepared (standards are set by the **Accounting Standards Board**) and

- the review of financial statements that have already been published (by the **Financial Reporting Review Panel**).

It also has responsibility for the following regulatory functions:

- Issuing auditing standards – through the Auditing Practices Board (APB)

- Oversight of the accountancy profession – through the Professional Oversight Board (POB)

- Investigation and discipline – through the Accountancy and Actuarial Discipline Board (AADB)

The structure of the FRC is shown in the diagram below:

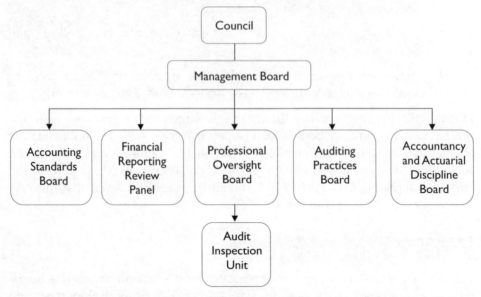

The role of the **Professional Oversight Board (POB)** is to provide:

(i)   Independent oversight of the regulation of the auditing profession by the recognised supervisory and qualifying bodies

(ii)   Monitoring of the quality of the auditing function in relation to economically significant entities

(iii)   Independent oversight of the regulation of the accountancy profession by the professional accountancy bodies

(iv)   Independent oversight of the regulation of the actuarial profession

The **Auditing Practices Board (APB),** as its name suggests, acts mainly in relation to audit practices. In particular this involves establishing high standards in auditing, meeting the developing needs of users of financial information and ensuring public confidence in the audit process.

The **Audit Inspection Unit** carries out inspections and reviews of the audits of listed companies.

The **Accountancy and Actuarial Discipline Board** acts as a tribunal for disciplinary hearings, and can impose fines and other sanctions against accountants whose work fails to measure up to professional standards.

Task 6

Which organisation of the Financial Reporting Council (FRC) acts as an independent body responsible for monitoring the regulation of the accountancy profession by the professional accountancy bodies?

	✓
The Financial Reporting Review Panel (FRRP)	
The Accounting Standards Board (ASB)	
The Professional Oversight Board (POB)	

There is a strong, growing international dimension to the regulation of the accountancy profession. The FRC oversees the profession in the UK, but while approaches differ across the world, national regulators increasingly share their ideas and practices, especially within the European Union.

There is also global convergence of accounting and auditing standards, which means that bodies such as the APB need to work with their counterparts from other countries. This work is carried out by international bodies such as the IAASB (International Auditing and Assurance Standards Board), which is part of IFAC (International Federation of Accountants).

The International Federation of Accountants (IFAC)

Sections 1.2 and 1.3 of the AAT Guidelines state:

They [the Guidelines] are based on the *Code of Ethics for Professional Accountants* approved by the **International Federation of Accountants** (IFAC) in June 2005. The AAT is an associate member of IFAC. The mission of IFAC, as set out in its constitution, is "the worldwide development and enhancement of an accountancy profession with harmonised standards, able to provide services of consistently high quality in the public interest."

In pursuing this mission, the IFAC Board has established the IFAC Ethics Committee to develop and issue, under its own authority, high quality ethical standards and other pronouncements for members for use around the world. The *IFAC Code of Ethics* on which these *Guidelines* are based establishes ethical requirements for IFAC members.

In keeping with the IFAC Code, these *Guidelines* adopt a **principles-based approach**. They do not attempt to cover every situation where a member may encounter professional ethical issues, prescribing the way in which he or she should respond. Instead, they adopt a value system, focusing on fundamental professional and ethical principles which are at the heart of proper professional behaviour and which members must therefore follow. To supplement this, the *Guidelines* also provide detailed guidance of specific relevance to AAT members to help ensure that they follow the fundamental principles both in word and in spirit in all of their professional activities.

IFAC is an **international body** representing all the **major accountancy bodies** across the world. Its mission is to develop the high standards of professional accountants and enhance the quality of services they provide.

IFAC's mission is to:

- Serve the public interest
- Strengthen the worldwide accountancy profession
- Establish and promote adherence to high quality professional standards
- Promote further international convergence of these standards

To enable the development of high standards, IFAC's ethics committee established a **code of ethics**, which has aligned standards globally. All of the main accountancy bodies in the world are required to comply with its principles. The code has the aim of identifying the responsibilities that a person employed as an accountant takes on, in return for a traditionally well paid career with high status. The code identifies potential situations where pitfalls may exist and offers advice on how to deal with them. By doing this the code indicates a minimum level of conduct that all accountants must adhere to.

The Consultative Committee of Accountancy Bodies (CCAB)

The major chartered accountancy professional bodies in the UK and Ireland joined together to form the **Consultative Committee of Accountancy Bodies**. CCAB has six members:

- The Institute of Chartered Accountants in England and Wales (ICAEW)
- The Institute of Chartered Accountants of Scotland (ICAS)
- The Institute of Chartered Accountants in Ireland (ICAI)
- The Association of Chartered Certified Accountants (ACCA)
- The Chartered Institute of Management Accountants (CIMA)
- The Chartered Institute of Public Finance and Accountancy (CIPFA)

CCAB provides a forum in which matters affecting the profession can be discussed and co-ordinated, and enables the profession to speak with a unified voice.

The AAT itself is not part of the CCAB.

The AAT is a qualification and membership body for accounting staff. The qualifications of the AAT are vocational; members are accounting technicians who have practical accounting skills for use in the workplace. The qualification then allows a vocational progression route to the UK's chartered and certified accountancy qualifications, including those of ACCA.

It is worth noting that four of the bodies that make up the CCAB – ICAEW, ICAS, CIMA and CIPFA – are sponsoring bodies of the AAT.

Financial Services Authority (FSA)

The Financial Services Authority (FSA) is an independent non-governmental body, given statutory powers by the Financial Services and Markets Act 2000. It is an independent body that regulates the financial services industry in the UK, including the running of investment businesses.

Forms of regulation

Regulation is defined as the controlling of behaviour (individual or the organisation) by rules or restrictions. It can take many forms, including legal restrictions imposed by the government, and self-regulation by an industry (such as with the accountancy profession). Breach of regulations can result in sanctions such as fines, but note that this does not necessarily mean that a criminal offence has taken place.

Common forms of regulation include the following.

Self-regulation

Self-regulation is the process whereby an organisation or industry monitors its own adherence to legal, ethical, or safety standards, rather than have an independent agency such as a government entity monitor and enforce those standards. This is the model largely adopted by the accountancy profession in the UK.

Independent watchdogs

The term 'watchdog' is an informal name usually given to consumer protection organisations or campaigners. These bodies are set up to monitor and campaign for standards in particular industries.

Ombudsman

An ombudsman is a person who acts as an intermediary between an organisation and external interests such as the general public. You may have heard of the Financial Ombudsman who helps settle disputes between consumers and their banks or other providers of financial services.

Government regulation

This is regulation put into place by the government or government controlled organisations. Common examples of this form of regulation include controls on prices, wages, pollution effects, employment, standards of production and standards of service.

CODES OF CONDUCT AND CODES OF PRACTICE

When considering the control of ethical behaviour, codes of conduct and codes of practice are often mentioned. We shall now consider the differences between the two.

Code of conduct (employee ethics)

A **code of conduct** is designed to influence the behaviour of employees: it sets out the procedures to be used in specific ethical situations – such as conflicts of interest or the acceptance of gifts, and the procedures to determine whether a violation occurred and what remedies should be imposed. The effectiveness of such codes depends on the extent to which management supports them. Violations of a code of conduct may make the violator subject to the organisation's sanctions, which could even result in the termination of employment.

Code of practice (professional ethics)

A **code of practice** is adopted by a profession or organisation to regulate its members, and provide clear guidance on what behaviour is considered ethical in the circumstances. In a membership context, failure to comply with a code of practice can result in expulsion from the professional organisation. The AAT's Guidelines is an example of a code of practice.

Codes of conduct and practice often have a special legal status. They are **not legally binding** on employees and members – only legislation can do that. But if a company is being prosecuted, for example for breaking health and safety law, and it can be shown that its organisation's code of practice was not followed, then the court is more likely to find the company at fault.

Put more simply, codes of practice are used in support of legal duties and offer practical examples of good practice. They are not pieces of law in themselves but give advice on how to comply with the law.

BUSINESS ETHICS AND PROFESSIONAL VALUES

The concept of **business ethics** suggests that businesses are morally responsible for their actions, and should be held accountable for the effects of their actions on people and society. This is true for individual businesses and for 'business' in general, which has a duty to behave responsibly in the interests of the society of which it is a part.

In 'Setting the tone: ethical business leadership' by Philippa Foster Back (published by the Institute of Business Ethics) the author lists some business values as truth, transparency, fairness, responsibility and trust.

The importance of business values in a company's culture is that they underpin both policy and behaviour throughout the company, from top to bottom.

Managers usually have a duty to aim for profit. At the same time, modern ethical standards require them to protect the rights of a range of groups inside and outside the organisation who have a legitimate interest or 'stake' in the organisation's activities. These groups are often known as **stakeholders**.

Business ethics are also relevant to **competitive behaviour**: there is a distinction between competing aggressively and competing unethically (for example, by stealing competitors' designs; using buyer power to prevent suppliers from dealing with competitors; or spreading false negative information about competitors).

A consequence of the need for a business to act ethically is for it to **change its culture** so all employees, managers and directors know what is expected of them. For example, management might 'turn a blind eye' to employees submitting inflated expense claims, but this is not something an ethical organisation would allow, so the attitude of employees and mangers must be changed so that only accurate expense claims are made

To achieve this a **code of conduct** must be developed and 'sold' to the organisation.

Effective ethical programmes and codes of conduct

There are three elements to creating an effective ethical programme for a business:

Active leadership (setting the 'tone at the top')

The programme should be supported by the very top of the organisation. A senior board member should be appointed as 'Ethical Champion', whose initial role is to persuade all other senior executives to lead by example.

Buy-in

The Champion's next role is to organise a consultation process with members of staff to achieve their 'buy-in' to the new ethical culture. All staff should understand that the ethical code gives them principles and values that should be reflected in their everyday activities, and will help them deal with any ethical issues they come across while at work.

Training

Once employees understand the need for ethical behaviour and embrace the change in culture, training should be provided to ensure that all understand what is expected of them, and to further instil the ethical message. Helplines may be set up to provide employees with advice for dealing with ethical problems.

Benefits of a code of conduct

Organisations that develop and introduce codes of conduct find a number of benefits from doing so, these include:

Communication

Ethical codes communicate the standard of behaviour expected of employees and help them make the right choice between alternative courses of action.

Consistency of conduct

With the ethical message effectively communicated, the behaviour of employees can be standardised or made consistent across all operations and locations. Customers, suppliers and other stakeholders will receive similar treatment wherever they are.

Risk reduction

Standardised behaviour reduces the risk of unethical actions, as employees who are unethical will 'stand out' and can be dealt with. This reduces the risk of a few employees irrevocably damaging the reputation of the organisation and the trust people have in it.

Compliance with UK Corporate Governance

Corporate governance is concerned with rules and controls on how businesses are run. These rules and controls are usually put in place by the directors of a company. However, in recent years, non-legal guidance has been developed by the FRC that certain organisations (particularly those listed on the London Stock Exchange) should comply with or explain in their financial statements why they have not.

This guidance recommends that businesses draw up codes of conduct. The purpose is to ensure employees know what is expected of them.

THE 'I DO BEST' MODEL

An individual's ethical decisions could also be stated as answering the question: 'What can **I do** for the **best**?' The table below summarises this.

Element	Explanation
I	Ethics concern an individual's professional responsibility to act (*not* what might happen if you get caught!).
DO	Ethics concern the 'real world' practical actions an individual can take. It is important to consider *how* an individual acts, and not always *what* they do.
BEST	Ethics concern choices between different courses of action. These may involve having to take a course of action merely because it is less unpalatable than another.

The Nolan Principles of Public Life

The Committee on Standards in Public Life is an advisory body of the UK government which was established in response to concerns that conduct by some politicians was unethical.

A report by the **Nolan Committee** established **The Seven Principles of Public Life** which are relevant to accountants as there are some similarities with the AAT's Fundamental Principles.

The seven principles are:

Integrity

Holders of public office should not place themselves under any financial or other obligation to outside individuals or organisations that might seek to influence them in the performance of their official duties.

Objectivity

In carrying out public business, including making public appointments, awarding contracts, or recommending individuals for rewards and benefits, holders of public office should make choices on merit.

Accountability

Holders of public office are accountable for their decisions and actions to the public and must submit themselves to whatever scrutiny is appropriate to their office.

Openness

Holders of public office should be as open as possible about all the decisions and actions that they take. They should give reasons for their decisions and restrict information only when the wider public interest clearly demands.

Honesty

Holders of public office have a duty to declare any private interests relating to their public duties and to take steps to resolve any conflicts arising in a way that protects the public interest.

Leadership

Holders of public office should promote and support these principles by leadership and example.

Selflessness

Holders of public office should act solely in terms of the public interest. They should not do so in order to gain financial or other material benefits for themselves, their family, or their friends.

Please note that leadership and selflessness are not really relevant to accountants; focus your attention on the other definitions.

Task 7

Which of the following is one of the Seven Principles of Public Life identified by the Nolan Committee?

	✓
Independence	
Openness	
Confidentiality	

RISKS FROM IMPROPER PRACTICE

There are a number of risks associated with doing business which mean that it is important for all employees, including accountants, to be vigilant. Maintaining an ethical stance in business dealings will help to ensure that a consistent approach is taken, and that as far as possible the effects of such risks can be minimised.

Operational risk

A particularly important risk is **operational risk**. This is defined by the **Basel Committee on Banking Supervision** (BCBS) as:

"The risk of loss resulting from inadequate or failed internal processes, people and systems or from external events."

An operational risk is therefore the risk of losses arising simply from the day-to-day business of the company – whether through its processes, its staff, its systems or from external events.

It is a broad concept including the risk of fraud, legal risks, physical and environmental risks. Risk management is usually carried out within the various business functions, and so it becomes an issue that affects every member of staff. For example, the IT department will take care of the risks associated with the processing, storage and use of information, and the human resources department will take care of personnel risks through its recruitment and selection procedures.

It is important to understand that the factors which contribute to operational risk (basically anything the organisation does in the conduct of its business) can be controlled to some extent by codes of conduct and an ethical programme. Therefore there is a link between good ethical safeguards and a reduction in operation risk and associated losses.

Types of operational risk

The following are the specific areas, listed by the Basel Committee, of operational risk for a business. Questions of ethics and ethical behaviour could arise in each one.

- Internal fraud
- External fraud
- Employment practices and workplace safety
- Clients, products and business practice
- Damage to physical assets
- Business disruption and systems failures
- Processes and delivery of outputs

Other types of operational risk include reputational risk and litigation risk.

Reputational risk is damage to an organisation through loss of its reputation. It can arise as a consequence of operational failures. So, for example, if a company performs poorly in answering calls at its customer service centre, because it does not employ enough staff, the reputation of the whole organisation could be tarnished.

Litigation risk is loss or damage which is the consequence of legal action or failure to follow a code of practice. For example, an organisation might have to pay damages to a customer for injuries caused to them by a faulty product.

Operational risk can also be classified into:

- Process risk – losses resulting from poorly designed business processes

- People risk – losses resulting from human error or deliberate actions

- Systems risk – losses resulting from poorly designed systems such as internal and external controls

- Legal risk – losses resulting from failure to adhere to legal requirements

- Event risk – losses from one-off or on-going incidents such as a fire in a factory or the collapse of a market for the organisation's products

Types of event risk

Event risk is the operational risk of loss due to single events that are unlikely but may have serious consequences. Natural or man-made disasters are the most obvious examples of event risk. These may include:

- Disaster risk: a catastrophe occurs, such as fire, flood, ill health or death of key people, terrorism and so on

- Regulatory risk: new laws or regulations are introduced, affecting the business's operations and profitability

- Reputation risk: mentioned above in terms of ongoing activity, the business's activities in relation to a single event could also damage its reputation in the eyes of stakeholders.

- Systemic risk: the system itself is put at risk by an event, e.g. by failure of a participant in the business's supply chain or system to meet its contractual obligations

Another way of classifying event risks is according to their sources in the external environment:

- Physical risks: such as climate and geology

- Social risks: changes in tastes, attitudes and demography

- Political risks: changes determined by government, or by a change of government

- Legal risks: changes in legislation and regulations, including the consequences of breaking the law or otherwise failing to meet legal duties or obligations

- Economic risks: changing economic conditions

- Operating environment risks: technological changes

Risk and accountants

All operational risks are real issues for accountants but there are safeguards in place to help reduce them. For example, following the due diligence rules set out in the AAT's Guidelines (s 210.4) when new clients are taken on will help reduce operational risk related to business practice. These relate specifically to money laundering and we shall look at their detail in a later chapter.

Reputational and litigation risk are also consequences to individual accountants who act unethically. As we are about to see, litigation may be taken against AAT members for failure to follow the Guidelines, and this will impact on their personal and professional reputation.

Task 8

Damage to assets is an example of a loss resulting from which type of operational risk?

	✓
Reputational	
Litigation	
Physical	

AAT DISCIPLINARY REGULATIONS

We have considered above, the risks to an organisation of improper practice. There are also consequences for the individual accountant of non-compliance with codes of practice and regulations.

The AAT has a set of **Disciplinary Regulations for Members**, where it defines misconduct by a member as follows:

"[having] conducted him/herself in such a manner as would in the opinion of the Investigations Team or the Disciplinary Tribunal, as applicable, prejudice his/her status as a member or reflect adversely on the reputation of the Association".

Regulations 7 to 11 covering who can make a complaint and the possible grounds for action against a member are summarised below.

Who can make a complaint?

7   Any person may make a complaint in writing to the Association concerning the conduct of a member.

8   The Association shall consider and, where appropriate, investigate complaints made within a reasonable period.

9   The Association itself may commence proceedings if it becomes aware of matters concerning the conduct of a member which in its opinion warrants inquiry.

Grounds for Disciplinary Action

10   Grounds for disciplinary action will exist if a member conducts themselves in a manner which prejudices their status as a member or reflects adversely on the reputation of the Association. This includes acting in serious or repeated breach of the rules of the Association.

11   The following events are deemed conclusive proof of misconduct:

(i)   a member pleads guilty to or has been found guilty of an indictable criminal offence;

(ii)   a member becomes bankrupt or enters into any formal arrangement with their creditors;

(iii)   a member unreasonably refuses to co-operate with an investigation into their conduct;

(iv)   a member repeatedly fails to reply to correspondence from the Association.

It is a duty of every member to inform the Association of any event listed above that involves themselves. Failure to do this is construed as conclusive proof of misconduct.

The Disciplinary Process

The **Disciplinary Process** has four stages:

Stage 1   **Disciplinary investigation** to establish the facts

Stage 2   **Decision and recommendation** as to whether there are grounds for action

Stage 3   **Member's response** to those recommendations

Stage 4   **Disciplinary Tribunal** to hear submissions and witnesses

The following disciplinary actions may be recommended for a member who is found guilty of misconduct:

- Be expelled from the Association
- Have his/her membership of the Association suspended
- Have his/her practising Licence withdrawn
- Be declared ineligible for a practising Licence
- Have his/her fellow member status removed
- Be severely reprimanded
- Be reprimanded
- Be fined a sum not exceeding such maximum figure as the Council may set from time to time
- Give a written undertaking to refrain from continuing or repeating the misconduct in question

CONTINUING PROFESSIONAL DEVELOPMENT (CPD)

Continuing Professional Development (CPD) has a crucial role in ensuring that you maintain your **technical** and **professional competence**, keeping pace with changes in your work role and the practices, techniques and standards of your profession.

130.3 The maintenance of **professional competence** requires continuing awareness and understanding of relevant technical, professional and business developments. **Continuing professional development** develops and maintains the capabilities that enable a member to perform competently within the professional environment. To achieve this, Council has recommended a programme of relevant CPD which is output based. This requires members to assess, plan, action and evaluate their learning and development needs.

It is a condition of AAT membership that each AAT member completes a four-step CPD cycle at least once a year.

This four-step cycle consists of:

- Assessing your learning and development needs for the year (or half-year) ahead

- Planning the learning activity you will undertake

- Putting the learning plan into action

- Evaluating the outcomes at the end of the year (or half-year)

Members who provide services on a self-employed basis must register on the AAT's Scheme for Members in Practice and comply with the associated guidelines (AAT's Guidelines s200.3).

HOW IT WORKS

Some training needs will emerge in the course of your work. If your organisation introduces new equipment or software, you may need to learn how to use it! You may also identify your own shortcomings (missed deadlines, subjects on which you had to get help from others, times when you did not get the results you wanted) as learning opportunities.

Training needs may also be identified for you, as you get informal performance feedback from your supervisors and colleagues – or through formal appraisal interviews.

Other training needs may be identified as you keep in touch with developments in your professional environment: through the internet, professional journals (such as Accounting Technician), and networking opportunities through your professional body.

There is a huge menu of learning resources and opportunities available for you to use in order to meet you training needs, including:

- Courses, workshops and information seminars

- Books, quality newspapers, professional journals and technical publications (such as accounting standards, legislation and court reports)

- Videos, CD-ROM and computer software packages for education and training

- Web sites (for information and accessing training and materials)

- Instruction and procedure manuals used in your organisation (e.g. to teach you to use equipment and software, or to comply with organisational procedures and practices)

And there are two other very valuable sources of learning:

- **Other people**

  Your superiors and colleagues at work are an excellent potential source of information, advice and instruction/coaching in areas where they are more expert or experienced than you are. They may be able to help you access opportunities (eg nominating you for training programmes or secondments). They are also in an ideal position to offer you feedback (about your strengths and weaknesses, learning/improvement needs and how you are doing in your learning).

  Professional networks provide similar support and guidance within your wider professional sphere.

- **Your own experience**

  'Doing something' is an important development technique! Identify opportunities to try a new technique or approach at work, which you could use as a learning opportunity. If you want to learn to contribute more effectively to meetings, for example, what meetings could you arrange to participate in and observe? Whom could you ask for feedback?

 Signpost

See the AAT Guidelines on Professional Ethics:

ss1.11, 100.4, 100.12, 130.3 and 200.3

Task 9

If you ignore the AAT's rules on Continuing Professional Development you will be in breach of its Guidelines on Professional Ethics and therefore liable for a fine under criminal law.

	✔
True	
False	

CHAPTER OVERVIEW

- **Ethical values** are assumptions and beliefs about what constitutes 'right' and 'wrong' behaviour. Individuals, families, national cultures and organisation cultures all develop ethical values and norms

- **Ethical behaviour** is necessary to comply with law and regulation; to protect the public interest; to protect the reputation and standing of a professional body and its members; and to enable people to live and work together in society

- The **AAT's Guidelines on Professional Ethics** note that: 'the decisions you make in the everyday course of your professional lives can have real ethical implications'

- **The five fundamental principles** in an accounting context are:
  - Integrity
  - Objectivity
  - Professional competence and due care
  - Confidentiality and
  - Professional behaviour

- The AAT Guidelines on Professional Ethics set out a **basic problem solving procedure** for unethical action (the 'conceptual framework'):
  - Identify the threat to the fundamental principles that the action represents
  - Evaluate the threat
  - Apply safeguards to eliminate or reduce the threat
  - If safeguards cannot be applied, decline or discontinue the action

- The **principles-based approach** to ethics encourages case-by-case judgement

- The accountancy profession is largely self-regulatory, with the professional accountancy bodies each responsible for setting and upholding the ethical standards of their members. This chapter looked at:
  - FRC
  - IFAC
  - CCAB
  - FSA

- A **code of conduct** is designed to influence the behaviour of employees; it sets out the procedures to be used in specific ethical situations

- A **code of practice** is adopted by a profession or organisation to regulate that profession

- Ethics could be stated as answering the question: '**What can I do for the best?**'

- The concept of **business ethics** suggests that businesses and other corporate entities are morally responsible for their actions

- Key issues in being an **ethical employee and colleague** include: not undertaking tasks that are beyond your personal experience and expertise; not undermining your professional colleagues; honesty; and ethical relationships

- The **Basel Committee on Banking Supervision** has provided the following definition of operational risk; "The risk of loss resulting from inadequate or failed internal processes, people and systems or from external events."

- The AAT has issued its own **Disciplinary Regulations for Members and defines misconduct as behaving;** "..in such a manner as would in the opinion of the Investigations Team or the Disciplinary Tribunal, as applicable, prejudice his/her status as a member or reflect adversely on the reputation of the Association".

- **Continuing Professional Development** activities ensure that you maintain your technical and professional competence, keeping pace with changes in your work role and the practices, techniques and standards of your profession

- CPD involves both **formal and informal** learning experiences

TEST YOUR LEARNING

Respond **to the following by selecting the appropriate option.**

Test 1

Only individuals can have 'ethical values'.

	✓
True	
False	

Test 2

The AAT needs to protect its reputation and standing by maintaining standards of conduct and service among its members in order to be able to:

	✓
Enhance the reputation and standing of its members	
Limit the number of members that it has	
Make sure that its members are able to earn large salaries	

Test 3

Which of these might (or might be thought to) affect the objectivity of providers of professional accounting services?

	✓
Failure to keep up to date on CPD	
A personal financial interest in the client's affairs	
Being negligent or reckless with the accuracy of the information provided to the client	

Test 4

A client asks you a technical question about accounting standards which you are not sure you are able to answer correctly. 'You are supposed to be an accountant, aren't you?' says the client. 'I need an answer now.' What should you do first?

	✔
Say that you will get back to him when you have looked up the answer	
Give him the contact details of a friend in your firm who knows all about accounting standards	
Clarify the limits of your expertise with the client	

Test 5

Put the four steps of the problem-solving methodology or 'conceptual framework' for ethical conduct into the correct order:

Apply safeguards to eliminate or reduce the threat to an acceptable level	
Evaluate the seriousness of the threat	
Discontinue the action or relationship giving rise to the threat	
Identify a potential threat to a fundamental ethical principle	

Test 6

Why are professional standards important?

	✔
It is in the public interest that employees who fail to comply with standards are prosecuted	
It is in the public interest that services are carried out to professional standards	

Test 7

Which of the following are member boards of the Financial Reporting Council?

	✓
Accounting Standards Board	
International Federation of Accountants	
Consultative Committee of Accountancy Bodies	
Financial Reporting Review Panel	
Professional Oversight Board	
Auditing Practices Board	
Financial Services Authority	
Accountancy and Actuarial Discipline Board	

Test 8

The Basel Committee on Banking Supervision defines operational risk as: "the risk of loss resulting from inadequate or failed internal processes, people and systems or from ..."

	✓
External events	
Government regulation	

Test 9

Which of the following are counted amongst the Nolan Principles on standards in public life?

	✓
Diplomacy	
Selflessness	
Honesty	
Legality	
Accuracy	
Objectivity	
Accountability	
Leadership	

Test 10

An AAT member who is found guilty of misconduct may be fined an unlimited amount.

	✓
True	
False	

chapter 2:
BEHAVING IN AN ETHICAL MANNER I

chapter coverage 📖

AAT Members may work for a commercial organisation in business or in practice with an accountancy firm. This means they perform a range of roles from processing invoices to preparing and reporting financial and other information, which their employer and third parties may rely on. They may also be responsible for financial management and advice on a range of business-related matters.

In this and the next chapter we shall build on the ethical principles which were introduced in Chapter 1 and identify how they should be applied in practice.

As you saw earlier, the AAT's Guidelines has sections which are directly applicable to members in business and in practice. Where possible we shall consider the rules applicable to each type of member together. Remember, you should be aware of all the rules, not just the ones applicable to your current role.

The topics we cover are:

✍ Acting with integrity, honesty, fairness and sensitivity

✍ Safeguards to protect against threats to fundamental principles

✍ Acquiring and working with clients

ACTING WITH INTEGRITY, HONESTY, FAIRNESS AND SENSITIVITY

You should have realised from Chapter 1 that accounting matters often require the use of personal judgement and opinions as to the best or 'right' way to handle them can sincerely differ. Moreover, people need to develop their own ethical and technical judgement, as part of their own personal and continuing professional development. We shall now look at what behaving ethically means in practice beginning with acting with integrity, honesty, fairness and sensitivity in your dealings with clients, suppliers, colleagues and others.

Integrity

Accountants have a key role in preparing **financial statements**. Members in business may also prepare and report on a range of **information** for use by management and others – for example forecasts and budgets, costings, pricing calculations and management/business reports.

There is a clear need to apply the principles of integrity (not presenting untruthful or misleading information), confidentiality (not disclosing confidential information), competence and due care (preparing and presenting information in accordance with financial reporting and other applicable professional standards) and objectivity (presenting information free of bias or self interest).

Section 320 of the AAT Guidelines state:

320.1 Members in business are often involved in the preparation and reporting of information that may either be made public or used by others inside or outside the employing organisation. Such information may include financial or management information, for example, forecasts and budgets, financial statements, management discussion and analysis and the management letter of representation provided to the auditors as part of an audit of financial statements. A member in business should prepare or present such information **fairly**, **honestly** and **in accordance with relevant professional standards** so that the information will be understood in its context.

320.2 A member in business who has responsibility for the preparation or approval of the general purpose financial statements of an employing organisation should ensure that those financial statements are presented in accordance with the **applicable financial reporting standards**.

320.3 A member in business should **maintain information** for which the member in business is responsible in a manner that

(i)   describes clearly the **true nature of business transactions, assets** or **liabilities**

(ii) **classifies** and **records information accurately** and in a **timely** and proper manner

(iii) **represents** the **facts accurately** and **completely** in all material respects.

320.4 Threats to compliance with the **fundamental principles**, for example self-interest or intimidation threats to objectivity or professional competence and due care, may be created as a result of pressure to become associated with misleading information. This pressure may arise externally or by the possibility of personal gain and by the member's own actions or by the actions of others.

320.5 The **significance** of such **threats** will depend on factors such as the source of the pressure and the degree to which the information is, or may be, misleading. The significance of the threats must be evaluated and, if they are not clearly insignificant, safeguards must be considered and applied as necessary to eliminate them or reduce them to an acceptable level. Such safeguards may include consultation with superiors within the employing organisation, for example, the audit committee or other body responsible for governance, or with a relevant professional body.

320.6 Where it is not possible to **reduce the threat** to an acceptable level, a member in business should **refuse to remain associated with information** they consider is or may be misleading. Should the member in business be aware that the issuance of misleading information is either significant or persistent, the member in business should consider informing appropriate authorities in line with the guidance in Section 140. The member in business may also wish to seek legal advice or resign.

 Signpost

See the AAT Guidelines on Professional Ethics:

- Section 320: Preparing and reporting information

Honesty

Honesty simply means being truthful and not acting in a manner intended to mislead or deceive others. Using the work phone for personal calls when not permitted and taking 'sick days' when you are not sick are fairly common behaviours – and your organisation's culture may have come to regard them as 'harmless' or even 'normal'. But they are still dishonest. Just because 'everyone does it' does not make it right.

Task 1

List some examples of behaviours that would be considered dishonest for you either as a student of the AAT or as an employee in a work context. Include an example of dishonest behaviour that the perpetrator might not even be aware was dishonest.

Fairness

Acting fairly means treating others equally. The increasing diversity of the modern workplace requires fairness, mutual respect and open communication, as the basis for constructive working relationships. As an accountant you not only have an ethical reason to be fair, but there is legislation in the UK which prohibits discrimination and harassment on a variety of grounds. These include race and colour, sex and sexual orientation, and religious belief.

Sensitivity

Sensitivity essentially means respecting another's right to confidentiality and privacy. Employers have specific duties to respect the confidentiality of employee information, but this should be extended to individual relationships – particularly if you have authority over others (and may be involved in counselling, disciplinary or grievance interviews).

SAFEGUARDS TO PROTECT AGAINST THREATS TO FUNDAMENTAL PRINCIPLES

We saw in Chapter 1 that the AAT's Guidelines identify a number of threats to its fundamental principles and some safeguards designed to protect against such threats. To recap, the threats identified are:

- Self-interest
- Self-review
- Familiarity
- Intimidation
- Advocacy

Since members who work in an accountancy practice are affected by different threats to those working in a commercial business, the guidelines make specific recommendations to each situation.

The guidelines go into considerable detail which is set out below. However there are two tables which follow that summarise a number of important threats and safeguards for each type of member.

Members in practice

The AAT Guidelines (Part B) provide the following:

200.6 Examples of circumstances that may create **self-interest threats** for a member in practice include, but are not limited to:

(i)   a **financial interest** in a **client** or jointly holding a financial interest with a client

(ii)   **undue dependence** on **total fees** from a **client**

(iii) having a **close business relationship** with a **client**

(iv)   **concern** about the **possibility** of **losing** a **client**

(v)   **potential employment** with a **client**

(vi)   **contingent fees** relating to an **assurance engagement**

(vii) a **loan** to or from an **assurance client** or any of its **directors** or **officers**.

200.7 Examples of circumstances that may create **self-review threats** include, but are not limited to:

(i)   the **discovery** of a **significant error** during a re-evaluation of the work of the member in practice

(ii)   **reporting** on the operation of **financial systems** after being **involved** in their **design** or **implementation**

(iii) having **prepared** the **original data** used to generate records that are the subject matter of the engagement

(iv)   a member of the assurance team being, or having **recently been**, a **director** or **officer** of that **client**

(v)   a member of the assurance team being, or having recently been, employed by the client in a **position** to **exert direct** and **significant influence** over the subject matter of the engagement

(vi)   performing a service for a client that directly affects the **subject matter** of the assurance engagement.

200.8 Examples of circumstances that may create **advocacy threats** include, but are not limited to:

(i)   **promoting shares** in a listed entity when that entity is a financial statement audit client

(ii)   **acting as an advocate** on behalf of an assurance client in litigation or disputes with third parties.

200.9 Examples of circumstances that may create **familiarity threats** include, but are not limited to:

(i)   a member of the engagement team having a **close** or **personal relationship** with a director or officer of the client

(ii)   a member of the engagement team having a **close** or **personal relationship** with an employee of the client who is in a **position to**

> **exert direct** and **significant influence** over the subject matter of the engagement
>
> (iii) a **former partner** of the firm being a director or officer of the client or an employee in a position to exert direct and significant influence over the subject matter of the engagement
>
> (iv) **accepting gifts** or **preferential treatment** from a client, unless the value is clearly insignificant

(v) long association of senior personnel with the assurance client.

200.10 Examples of circumstances that may create **intimidation threats** include, but are not limited to:

> (i) being **threatened with dismissal** or **replacement** in relation to a client engagement

> (ii) being **threatened with litigation**

> (iii) being **pressured** to **reduce inappropriately** the **quality** or **extent of work** performed in order to reduce fees.

200.11 A member in practice may also find that **specific circumstances** give rise to unique threats to compliance with one or more of the fundamental principles. Such unique threats obviously cannot be categorised. In either professional or business relationships, a member in practice should always be on the alert for such circumstances and threats.

200.12 **Safeguards** that may eliminate or reduce threats to an acceptable level fall into two broad categories:

> (i) safeguards created by the **profession**, **legislation** or **regulation** and

> (ii) safeguards in the **work environment**.

Examples of safeguards created by the profession, legislation or regulation are described in paragraph 100.12 of Part A of these Guidelines.

200.13 In the work environment, the relevant safeguards will vary depending on the circumstances.

Work environment safeguards may be either **firm-wide safeguards** or safeguards which are specific to one particular engagement. A member in practice should in both cases exercise judgement to determine how to best deal with an identified threat. In exercising this judgement, a member in practice should consider what a reasonable and informed third party, having knowledge of all relevant information, including the significance of the threat and the safeguards applied, would reasonably conclude to be acceptable. This consideration will be affected by matters such as the significance of the threat, the nature of the engagement and the structure of the firm.

200.14 Firm-wide safeguards in the **work environment** may include:

(i) development of a **leadership culture** within the firm that stresses the importance of compliance with the fundamental principles

(ii) development of a leadership culture within the firm that establishes the **expectation that members** of an assurance team will **act in the public interest**

(iii) policies and procedures to implement and monitor **quality control of engagements**

(iv) documented **policies** regarding the **identification of threats** to **compliance** with the fundamental principles, the **evaluation** of the significance of these threats and the identification and the application of safeguards to eliminate or reduce the threats, other than those that are clearly insignificant, to an acceptable level

(v) for firms that perform assurance engagements, documented independence **policies** regarding the **identification of threats** to **independence**, the **evaluation** of the significance of these threats and the evaluation and application of safeguards to eliminate or reduce the threats, other than those that are clearly insignificant, to an acceptable level

(vi) documented **internal policies** and **procedures** requiring compliance with the fundamental principles

(vii) policies and procedures that will enable **the identification of interests** or **relationships** between the firm or members of engagement teams and clients

(viii) **policies** and **procedures** to **monitor** and, if necessary, **manage** the reliance on **revenue** received from a single client

(ix) using **different partners** and **engagement teams** with separate reporting lines for the provision of non-assurance services to an assurance client

(x) **policies** and **procedures** to **prohibit individuals** who are not members of an engagement team from inappropriately influencing the outcome of the engagement

(xi) **timely communication** of a firm's **policies** and **procedures**, including any changes to them, to all partners and professional staff, and appropriate training and education on such policies and procedures

(xii) designating a member of **senior management** to be responsible for **overseeing** the adequate functioning of the firm's **quality control system**

(xiii)   advising partners and professional staff of those assurance clients and related entities from which they must be **independent**

(xiv)   a **disciplinary mechanism** to promote compliance with policies and procedures

(xv)   published **policies** and **procedures** to **encourage** and **empower staff** to **communicate** to senior levels within the firm any issue relating to compliance with the fundamental principles that concerns them.

200.15 Engagement-specific **safeguards** in the **work environment** may include:

(i)   involving an **additional member** to review the work done or otherwise advise as necessary

(ii)   **consulting an independent third party**, such as a committee of independent directors, a professional regulatory body or another member

(iii)   **discussing ethical issues** with those charged with governance of the client

(iv)   **disclosing** to those charged with governance of the client the **nature of services** provided and **extent of fees** charged

(v)   **involving another firm** to perform or re-perform part of the engagement

(vi)   **rotating** senior assurance team **personnel**.

200.16 Depending on the nature of the engagement, a member in practice may also be able to **rely on safeguards that the client has implemented**. However it is not possible to rely solely on such safeguards to reduce threats to an acceptable level.

200.17 **Safeguards** within the **client's systems** and procedures may include:

(i)   when a client appoints a member in practice or a firm to perform an engagement, where appropriate persons other than management **ratify** or **approve** the appointment

(ii)   the client has **competent employees** with experience and seniority to make managerial decisions

(iii)   the client has implemented **internal procedures** that ensure **objective choices** in commissioning non-assurance engagements

(iv)   the client has a **corporate governance structure** that provides appropriate oversight and communications regarding the firm's services.

Members in business

The AAT Guidelines (Part C) provide the following:

300.8 Examples of circumstances that may create **self-interest threats** for a member in business include, but are not limited to:

(i)   **financial interests**, loans or guarantees
(ii) receipt of **incentive compensation arrangements**
(iii) inappropriate **personal use** of **corporate assets**
(iv) concern over **employment security**
(v)   **commercial pressure** from outside the employing organisation
(vi) **commissions**.

300.9 Circumstances that may create self-review threats include, but are not limited to, **business decisions** or **data** being **subject to review and justification by the same member** in business responsible for making those decisions or preparing that data.

300.10 When furthering the legitimate goals and objectives of their employing organisations members in business may **promote the organisation's position**, provided any statements made are neither false nor misleading. Such actions generally would not create an advocacy threat.

300.11 Examples of circumstances that may create **familiarity threats** include, but are not limited to:

(i)   a member in business in a **position to influence financial** or **non-financial reporting** or **business decisions** having a close or personal relationship, or an associate who is in a position to benefit from that influence

(ii) **long association with business contacts** influencing business decisions

(iii) **acceptance of a gift or preferential treatment**, unless the value is clearly insignificant.

300.12 Examples of circumstances that may create **intimidation threats** include, but are not limited to:

(i)   **threat of dismissal or replacement** of the member in business or their close or personal relation or associate over a disagreement about the application of an accounting principle or the way in which financial information is to be reported

(ii) a **dominant personality** attempting to **influence the decision making process**, for example with regard to the awarding of contracts or the application of an accounting principle.

300.13 Members in business may also find that **specific circumstances** give rise to unique threats to compliance with one or more of the fundamental principles. Such unique threats obviously cannot be categorised. In all professional and business relationships, members in business should always be on the alert for such circumstances and threats.

300.14 **Safeguards** that may eliminate or reduce to an acceptable level the threats faced by members in business fall into two broad categories:

    (i)   safeguards created by the **profession**, **legislation** or **regulation**

    (ii)   safeguards in the **work environment**.

300.15 Examples of safeguards created by the profession, legislation or regulation are detailed in paragraph 100.12 (regarding 'Safeguards created by the profession, legislation or regulation').

300.16 Safeguards in the **work environment** include, but are not restricted to:

    (i)   the **employing organisation's systems** of corporate oversight or other oversight structures

    (ii)   the **employing organisation's ethics** and **conduct programmes**

    (iii)   **recruitment procedures** in the employing organisation emphasising the importance of employing high calibre competent staff

    (iv)   strong **internal controls**

    (v)   appropriate **disciplinary processes**

    (vi)   **leadership** that stresses the importance of ethical behaviour and the expectation that employees will act in an ethical manner

    (vii)   **policies** and **procedures** to implement and monitor the **quality** of employee performance

    (viii)   **timely communication** of the employing organisation's policies and procedures, including any changes to them, to all employees and appropriate training and education on such policies and procedures

    (ix)   **policies** and **procedures** to empower and encourage employees to **communicate** to senior levels within the employing organisation any ethical issues that concern them without fear of retribution

    (x)   **consultation** with another appropriate professional.

300.17 There may be circumstances where a member in business believes that unethical behaviour or actions by others or by him or herself cannot be avoided or will continue to occur within the employing organisation. In such circumstances, the member in business should consider **seeking legal advice**. In those extreme situations where all available safeguards have been exhausted and it is not possible to reduce the threat to an acceptable level, a member in business may conclude that it is appropriate to resign from the employing organisation.

Key threats

The following table summarises some key threats to both types of member.

Threat	Members in practice	Members in business
Self-interest	■ Having a financial interest in a client ■ Depending upon a client's fees for a significant portion of your income ■ Having a close personal relationship with a client ■ Contingent fees relating to assurance work (these are fees that depend on the results of the work) ■ Receiving a loan from an assurance client	■ Having a financial interest (eg shares or a loan) in the employer ■ Financial incentives and rewards based on results or profits (including commission) ■ Opportunity to use corporate assets to your own advantage ■ Threats to your job security or promotion prospects ■ Commercial pressure (you need to help the firm compete and operate successfully, in order to keep your job)
Self-review	■ Discovery of a significant error when re-evaluating your work ■ Reporting on the operation of systems after being involved in designing them ■ Preparing the data which is used to generate reports which you are required to check ■ Being a recent employee of a business you are now auditing	■ Being asked to review data or justify/evaluate decisions that you have been involved in preparing/making
Familiarity	■ Having a close or personal relationship with a senior employee of a client ■ A former partner of a firm now employed in a senior position of the client so they are able to exert significant influence on the direction of the work	■ Having a close or personal relationship with someone who may benefit from your influence ■ Long association with a business contact, which may influence your decisions ■ Acceptance of a gift or preferential treatment, which

Threat	Members in practice	Members in business
	■ Accepting significant gifts from a client	might be thought to influence your decisions
Intimidation	■ Threat of dismissal, replacement, or litigation in respect of an engagement ■ Pressure to reduce the quality of your work in order to keep fees down	■ Threat of dismissal or other sanctions over a disagreement or a matter of ethical principle ■ A dominant individual attempting to influence your decisions
Advocacy	■ Promoting shares in a listed company which you audit ■ Acting on behalf of an audit client which is in a dispute with a third party	■ There is unlikely to be a significant advocacy threat to employees of an organisation. This is because they are entitled and expected to promote the employer's position or viewpoint, as part of furthering its legitimate goals and objectives.

Safeguards

The following table summarises some key safeguards available to both types of member.

Members in practice	Members in business
■ Development of a leadership culture in the firm that stresses the importance of compliance with the fundamental principles and acting in the public interest	■ Safeguards created by the profession, law and regulation (eg the AAT Ethical Guidelines or Money Laundering Regulations)
■ Policies and procedures to implement and monitor quality control and require compliance with the fundamental principles	■ The employer's structures and systems for corporate governance
■ Policies that identify threats to the fundament principles, evaluate their significance and identify safeguards to reduce or eliminate them	■ The employer's own ethical codes and disciplinary processes, and training/communication about them
■ Using different partners and teams to provide audit and non-audit services	■ Internal controls
■ Procedures that prevent non-team members influencing an engagement	■ Quality/performance monitoring systems
■ Communication of all policies and procedures and providing education and training in all policies and procedures	■ Recruitment, selection, appraisal, promotion, training and reward systems that all highlight ethics and competence as key criteria
■ Disciplinary procedures for failing to comply with policies and procedures	■ Leaders that communicate and model ethical behaviour and expectations
■ Engagement safeguards such as rotating audit teams, involving additional members or another firm to review work completed and consulting third parties for advice	■ Policies and procedures supporting employees in raising ethical concerns ('whistle blowing')
■ Reliance on safeguards in a client's system	■ Forums for discussing ethical issues at work (eg an ethics committee)
	■ The opportunity to consult with another professional (in confidence) if required

Task 2

An AAT member who works as part of an audit team having recently been a director or officer of the company they are auditing is likely to create which of the following threats?

	✓
Self-review	
Intimidation	
Advocacy	

 Signpost

See the AAT Guidelines on Professional Ethics:

- Section 200: Threats and safeguards (200.6 – 200.17)
- Section 300: Threats and safeguards (300.8 – 300.17)

ACQUIRING AND WORKING WITH CLIENTS

Acting with integrity, honesty and fairness does not just apply to the performance of your work as a member in business or in practice. There are a number of rules which relate to the acquisition of clients that members in practice must apply.

Professional appointment

For all sorts of reasons, a client may wish to change from one professional adviser to another. They may be relocating, or looking for more (or different) specialised expertise – or lower fees.

The key point to bear in mind when accepting a new appointment is to ensure that doing so does not breach any of the fundamental principles – in particular AAT members must not accept work which they are not competent to perform.

Clients have the right to change advisers. The ethical issue is how to protect the interests of all parties, by ensuring that information relevant to the change of appointment is properly exchanged.

The AAT Guidelines state:

210.1 Before **accepting a new client** relationship, a member in practice should consider whether acceptance would create any threats to compliance with the fundamental principles. Potential threats to integrity, objectivity, competence and due care, confidentiality or professional behaviour may be created by the characteristics and character of the client, or the nature of the client's business. For example, objectivity and professional behaviour could be compromised if the member has a close or personal relationship with the owners or managers of the client, or if the client aggressively presses the member for a particular outcome.

210.2 The **significance of any threats must be evaluated**. If identified threats are not clearly insignificant, safeguards must be considered and applied as necessary to eliminate them or reduce them to an acceptable level. The above examples could be largely dealt with by a comprehensive client engagement letter setting out the terms of the engagement and managing the client's expectations.

210.3 Quite separately from assessing the threat to compliance with the fundamental principles, the member in practice must **assess and mitigate the threat of the member's services being used to facilitate money laundering or terrorist financing**, in accordance with the applicable anti-money laundering legislation. The Money Laundering Regulations 2007 apply when: a member enters a professional relationship with a client, which the member estimates will have an element of duration; the member acts in relation to a transaction or series of related transactions amounting to 15,000 euro or more; or there is a suspicion of money laundering.

210.4 Where the above thresholds apply, the member must before entering the client relationship carry out adequate customer **due diligence** by:

(i) **identifying the client and verifying the client's identity** on the basis of documents, data or information obtained from a reliable source

(ii) where there is a beneficial owner who is not the client, **identifying the beneficial owner**, and taking adequate measures on a risk-sensitive basis to verify his or her identity so that the member is satisfied that he or she knows who the beneficial owner is, including in the case of a client that is a legal entity, measures to understand its ownership and control structure, and

(iii) **obtaining information** on the purpose and intended nature of the client relationship.

Members in practice must assess the risk of their services being used to facilitate money laundering or terrorist financing, taking into account the nature of the client and the client's business and apply the above measures in accordance with the perceived risk.

210.5 **Where it is not possible to complete adequate customer due diligence, a member in practice must decline to enter into the client relationship**. Where the member forms a suspicion that the client is engaged in money laundering or terrorist financing, the member must submit a report to the MLRO, if the member practices within a firm, or a Suspicious Activity Report to SOCA, if a sole practitioner. When sending a Suspicious Activity Report, a member may seek consent from SOCA to proceed with the client relationship. If a refusal is not received by the member within 7 working days, starting on the first working day after the consent request was made, consent is deemed. If a refusal is received within that 7 working days, then the member may continue with the client relationship or transaction after a further 31 days has elapsed, starting with the day on which the member received notice of the refusal, unless a restraining order is obtained to prohibit this. There is no deemed consent in relation to suspicions of terrorist financing.

210.6 All members have a responsibility to make themselves familiar with the applicable anti-money laundering and terrorist financing legislation and relevant guidance provided by the AAT.

What these rules effectively mean is that before accepting a new client, you should take into account any ethical problems that may arise as a consequence of it. For example, will you have the resources (staff, time, technical expertise) to give the client a quality service? Are there potential **threats to objectivity** (e.g. if you are related to an officer of the client company) or **confidentiality** (e.g. the client is a competitor of another client, and might pressure you to disclose information)?

Money laundering prevention procedures

You are also required, under the **Money Laundering Regulations 2007,** to exercise 'due diligence' in gathering information about a prospective customer, including:

- The client's **identity**, verified by appropriate identification and/or references – and the identity of the owner of the client (if separate)

- **'Know your client'** (**KYC**) information, including its expected patterns of business, its business model and its source of funds

Sufficient knowledge of a client must be maintained to enable you to identify unusual (and potentially suspicious) transactions. Where due diligence is not possible, you must decline to enter into relationship with the client. If you have any reasonable suspicion that the client may be engaged in money laundering or terrorist financing, you must report to the **Money Laundering Reporting Officer (MLRO)** of your firm (or **Serious Organised Crime Agency (SOCA)**, if you are a sole practitioner). We shall look at money laundering in more detail in a later chapter.

Transfer of clients

As well as acquiring new clients (and behaving ethically in respect of this), you may **receive a communication from a client**, saying that they want to transfer their business to another professional adviser. To behave ethically when ceasing to act for clients, the appropriate procedure is as follows:

Step 1   Respond promptly to all communications on the matter from your proposed successors.

Step 2   Disclose any issue or circumstance that might affect the successor's decision to accept the appointment – or confirm that there are no such issues.

In these circumstances, you may have to disclose matters that are damaging to the reputation of your client and any individuals concerned with their business. In UK law, this communication is generally protected by 'qualified privilege'. This means that you should not be liable if the client attempts to sue you for **defamation**. Defamation depends on the malicious use of untrue statements to damage someone's reputation – so in making your disclosure, be sure to state only what you believe to be true.

Another issue may arise if you suspect that the client is involved in money laundering: remember that you *cannot* make any disclosures that might be used to 'tip off' a possible money launderer or terrorist (we shall look at money laundering later on).

Step 3   Once the change of appointment has been made, hand over books and papers promptly to your successor if asked to do so. However, there may be an issue if you have exercised a lien over them, in pursuit of outstanding fees (we discuss this later on as well).

Step 4   If your successor needs other information from you, in the client's interests, give it promptly (and without charge – unless it involves a significant amount of work).

Recommendations and referrals

What about **recommendations and referrals**? A satisfied client may introduce others to your practice, and that's fine. You might also offer a **commission**, fee or reward to your employees for bringing in a new client. But you should never offer financial incentives to a third party to introduce clients (a referral fee or commission) – unless:

- The client is aware that the third party has been paid for the referral; and

- The third party is also bound by professional (or comparable) ethical standards, and can be trusted to carry out the introduction with integrity.

In the UK, if you receive a commission for introducing a client to another firm, and you are the client's agent or professional adviser you are legally bound to hand the money over to the client – unless they specifically approve your keeping it.

The AAT Guidelines state:

240.5 In certain circumstances, a member in practice may receive a **referral fee** or **commission** relating to a client. For example, where the member in practice does not provide the specific service required, a fee may be received for referring a continuing client to another member in practice or member of another IFAC member body or other expert. A member in practice may receive a commission from a third party (e.g. a software vendor) in connection with the sale of goods or services to a client.

240.6 A member who receives a commission or other reward in return for the introduction of a client should be aware that if such an introduction is made in the course of a **fiduciary relationship** with the client, the **member will be accountable** for the commission or reward to the client. That means that the member will, under UK and other common law regimes, be bound to pass over the commission or reward to the client, unless the latter, having been informed of the nature and amount of the commission or reward, agrees that the member can keep it. Accepting such a referral fee or commission may give rise to self-interest threats to objectivity and professional competence and due care.

240.7 A member in practice may also pay a **referral fee** to obtain a client, for example, where the client continues as a client of another member in practice or member of another IFAC member body but requires specialist services not offered by the existing accountant. The payment of such a referral fee may also **create a self-interest threat** to objectivity and professional competence and due care.

240.8 A member in practice should not pay or receive a referral fee or commission, unless the member in practice has established **safeguards** to eliminate the threats or reduce them to an acceptable level. Such safeguards may include:

(i) **disclosing** to the client any **arrangements to pay a referral fee** to another member in practice or member of another IFAC member body for the work referred

(ii) **disclosing** to the client any **arrangements to receive a referral fee** for referring the client to another member in practice

(iii) **obtaining advance agreement** from the client for commission arrangements in connection with the sale by a third party of goods or services to the client.

240.9 A member in practice may purchase all or part of another firm on the basis that payments will be made to individuals formerly owning the firm or to their heirs or estates. Such payments are not regarded as commissions or referral fees for the purpose of paragraphs 240.5 – 240.7 above.

What if you've just left an employer; can you try to 'take clients with you' to your new practice? The Guidelines suggest only that you should act 'professionally and with integrity', using your own judgement – but bear in mind the bad feeling that is likely to result.

Task 3

According to the AAT's Guidelines on Professional Ethics, before accepting any new client relationship, a member in practice should consider:

	✓
How profitable the relationship will be	
Whether acceptance would create any threats to compliance with the fundamental principles	
Whether the client's directors meet the firm's moral and ethical standards.	

Constraints on the services you can supply

Another point worth noting, is that for various reasons, you may not want to take on every client that approaches or is introduced to you! For example they may not offer sufficient profit or the work may be too specialised for your firm.

Additionally, the AAT's Guidelines include some constraints on the services members can supply, this is to protect against a member breaching the principle of professional competence and due care. The guidelines state:

210.7 **A member in practice should agree to provide only those services that the member in practice is competent to perform.** Before accepting a specific client engagement, a member in practice should consider whether acceptance would create any threats to compliance with the fundamental principles. For example, a self-interest threat to professional competence and due care is created if the engagement team does not possess, or cannot acquire, the competencies necessary to properly carry out the engagement.

210.8 **A member in practice must evaluate the significance of identified threats and, if they are not clearly insignificant, safeguards must be applied as necessary to eliminate them or reduce them to an acceptable level.** Such safeguards may include:

(i) **acquiring an appropriate understanding** of the nature of the client's business, the complexity of its operations, the specific requirements of the engagement and the purpose, nature and scope of the work to be performed

(ii) **acquiring knowledge of relevant industries** or subject matters

(iii) **possessing** or **obtaining experience** with relevant regulatory or reporting requirements

(iv) **assigning sufficient staff** with the necessary competencies

(v) **using experts** where necessary

(vi) agreeing on a **realistic time frame** for the performance of the engagement

(vii) **complying** with **quality control policies** and **procedures** designed to provide reasonable assurance that specific engagements are accepted only when they can be performed competently.

210.9 When a member in practice intends to **rely on the advice or work** of an expert, the member in practice should evaluate whether such reliance is warranted. The member in practice should consider factors such as reputation, expertise, resources available and applicable professional and ethical standards. Such information may be gained from prior association with the expert or from consulting others.

It is worth noting that as an accounting technician, there are certain services that you cannot legally offer unless you are authorised to do so by the relevant regulatory body in the UK. These include: **external audit** of UK limited companies, or where the services of a registered auditor are required; **investment business** (including agency for a building society) and the provision of corporate financial advice; and **insolvency practice.**

In addition, while you are providing public accountancy services, you should not at the same time engage in any other business, occupation or activity that:

- May threaten your **integrity**, **objectivity** or **independence**, or the reputation of the profession

- May prevent you from conducting your practice according to the technical and **ethical standards** of the profession

When considering accepting a particular engagement, you must also bear in mind any threat to the principle of **professional competence and due care**. You should only agree to provide services that you are competent to perform – or for which you can obtain the help, training or supervision you require in order to be able to perform competently.

Safeguards may include:

- Making sure that you have an adequate understanding of the client's business, and the specific requirements of the engagement

- Making sure that you have, or can obtain, relevant knowledge and experience, help or advice

- Consulting an expert, if required

- Making sure the timescales for the task are realistic (so you are not under undue time pressure)

Conflicts of interest

We looked briefly at what conflicts of interest are in Chapter 1 and the AAT Guidelines (Section 220) state a number of rules to deal with any conflicts as they arise:

220.1 A member in practice must take reasonable steps to identify circumstances that could pose a **conflict of interest.** Such circumstances may give rise to threats to compliance with the fundamental principles. For example, a threat to objectivity may be created when a member in practice competes directly with a client or has a joint venture or similar arrangement with a major competitor of a client. A threat to objectivity or confidentiality may also be created when a member in practice performs services for clients whose interests are in conflict or the clients are in dispute with each other in relation to the matter or transaction in question.

220.2 A member in practice must evaluate the significance of any threats. Evaluation includes considering, before accepting or continuing a client relationship or specific engagement, whether the member in practice has any business interests, or relationships with the client or a third party that could give rise to threats. If threats are not clearly insignificant, **safeguards** must be considered and applied as necessary to eliminate them or reduce them to an acceptable level.

220.3 Depending upon the circumstances giving rise to the conflict, safeguards should ordinarily include the member in practice:

(i) **notifying the client of the firm's business interest** or activities that may represent a conflict of interest, and obtaining their consent to act in such circumstances or

(ii) **notifying all known relevant parties** that the member in practice is acting for two or more parties in respect of a matter where their respective interests are in conflict, and obtaining their consent to so act, or

(iii) **notifying the client** that the member in practice does not **act exclusively** for any one client in the provision of proposed services (for example, in a particular market sector or with respect to a specific service) and obtaining their consent to so act.

220.4 Each of the following **additional safeguards** should also be considered:

(i) the use of **separate engagement teams**

(ii) **procedures to prevent access to information** (e.g. strict physical separation of such teams, confidential and secure data filing)

(iii) **clear guidelines** for members of the engagement team on issues of security and confidentiality

(iv) the use of **confidentiality agreements** signed by employees and partners of the firm, and

(v) **regular review of the application of safeguards** by a senior individual not involved with relevant client engagements.

220.5 Where a conflict of interest poses a threat to one or more of the fundamental principles, including objectivity, confidentiality or professional behaviour, that cannot be eliminated or reduced to an acceptable level through the application of safeguards, the member in practice should conclude that it is not appropriate to accept a specific engagement or that **resignation** from one or more conflicting engagements is required.

220.6 Where a member in practice has requested **consent** from a client to act for another party (which may or may not be an existing client) in respect of a matter where the respective interests are in conflict and that consent has been refused by the client, then they must not continue to act for one of the parties in the matter giving rise to the conflict of interest.

These rules essentially mean that when you accept a new appointment, or become aware of changes in the circumstances of an existing client, you should check whether this might create a conflict of interest with another client. The general principle is that the interests of one client must not have a negative effect on the interests of another.

An example would be if two client companies are in direct competition – and adverse disclosures or reports about one would benefit the other. Such conflicts create an ethical dilemma for the accountant, because it is impossible in such a case to act in the best interests of both clients at the same time – if you are required to make adverse disclosures about one of your clients, how is another, a competitor, to be expected to avoid making good use of them? It may also be an issue for a client, e.g. if they think there may be a risk that another client may (through the accountant) get hold of sensitive information.

If there is likely to be such a conflict of interest, you should:

- Put safeguards in place to avoid the negative effects, if possible

- Avoid new appointments that might negatively affect existing clients

- Disclose enough information to both parties, so that they can make a decision over whether to enter into (or continue) an engagement with you

In large firms, this may be less of a problem, as completely separate teams can work on different client accounts. (This is sometimes called 'building a **Chinese wall**' within the firm, between client affairs.)

Task 4

The situation where a firm of accountants has two clients which compete with each other is likely to create a conflict of interest for the accountant.

	✓
True	
False	

Second opinions

In some instances, a client of another firm may seek your opinion on the advice they have received from that firm. There are a large number of ethical issues that this raises, such as, is providing the advice fair to the other firm, or are you competent to do the work?

The AAT Guidelines state:

230.1 A member in practice may be asked to provide a **second opinion** on the application of accounting, auditing, reporting or other standards or principles to specific circumstances or transactions by or on behalf of a company or an entity that is not an existing client. This may give rise to threats to compliance with the fundamental principles. For example, there may be a threat to professional competence and due care in circumstances where the second opinion is not based on the same set of facts that were made available to the existing accountant, or is based on inadequate evidence. The significance of the threat will depend on the circumstances of the request and all the other available facts and assumptions relevant to the expression of a professional judgement.

230.2 When asked to provide such an opinion, a member in practice must **evaluate the significance of the threats**. Unless they are not clearly insignificant, safeguards must be considered and applied as necessary to eliminate them or reduce them to an acceptable level. Such safeguards may include seeking client permission to contact the existing accountant, describing the limitations surrounding any opinion in communications with the client and providing the existing accountant with a copy of the opinion.

230.3 If the company or entity seeking the opinion **will not permit communication** with the existing accountant, a member in practice should consider whether it is appropriate to provide the opinion sought, taking all the circumstances into account.

If a client approaches you to undertake work that is additional and related to the work of an existing professional adviser, you should similarly notify the existing adviser about this – unless the client can provide acceptable reasons for not doing so.

If you do not communicate with the other adviser(s), there may be a risk of duplicated effort (at best) and fraudulent or otherwise illegal activity (at worst).

There may also be a threat where you are asked to provide a second opinion on work done by another firm. Professional competence may be an issue, for example, if you do not have access to the same information that the other firm had. Again, getting permission to make contact with the other firm is one good safeguard.

Fees and remuneration

Accountants provide services for clients in return for fees which they usually charge on a time basis. This means the actual charges a client must pay are dependent on how much time the accountant takes to perform their work and how much they charge per hour. The ethical issues concerning fees are usually related to setting the hourly charge for different levels of staff and accurate time keeping. The AAT Guidelines state:

240.1 When entering into negotiations regarding professional services, a member in practice may **quote whatever fee is deemed to be appropriate**. The fact that one member in practice or member of another IFAC member body may quote a fee lower than another is not in itself unethical. Nevertheless, there may be threats to compliance with the fundamental principles arising from the level of fees quoted. For example, a self-interest threat to professional competence and due care is created if the fee quoted is so low that it may be difficult to perform the engagement in accordance with applicable technical and professional standards for that price.

240.2 The significance of such threats will depend on factors such as the level of fee quoted and the **services** to which it applies. In view of these potential threats, safeguards must be considered and applied as necessary to eliminate them or reduce them to an acceptable level. Safeguards which may be adopted include:

(i) making the client aware of the **terms of the engagement** and, in particular, the basis on which fees are charged and which services are covered by the quoted fee

(ii) assigning **appropriate time** and **qualified staff** to the task.

240.3 **Contingent fees** are widely used for certain types of non-assurance engagements. They may, however, give rise to threats to compliance with the fundamental principles in certain circumstances. They may give rise to a self-interest threat to objectivity. The significance of such threats will depend on factors including:

(i) the **nature of the engagement**

(ii) the **range of possible fee amounts**

(iii) the **basis for determining the fee**

(iv) whether the **outcome** or result of the transaction is to be **reviewed by an independent third party**.

240.4 The significance of such threats must be evaluated and, if they are not clearly insignificant, **safeguards** must be considered and applied as necessary to eliminate or reduce them to an acceptable level. Such safeguards may include:

(i) an **advance written agreement** with the client as to the basis of remuneration

(ii) **disclosure to intended users** of the work performed by the member in practice and the basis of remuneration

(iii) **quality control policies** and **procedures**

> (iv) **review by an objective third party** of the work performed by the member in practice.

As mentioned above, professional fees will normally be calculated on the basis of an agreed appropriate **rate per hour** or **per day** for the time of each person involved on the assignment. The 'appropriate rate' should take into account the skill, knowledge, experience, time and responsibility involved in the work. It also assumes that individuals give a 'fair hour's work for a fair hour's fees', in other words, that the work is efficiently planned and managed, so that clients get value for money. Note that there may be a threat to the principle of professional competence and due care if fees are set too *low*: it may be difficult to do a good job for that price!

It may not be possible to state accurately in advance what the total charge for work will be. If there is any likelihood that the fee will end up being substantially higher than you estimate, do not give the clients that estimate – or at least make it clear that the actual amount may be substantially higher.

It may, however, be necessary to charge a **pre-arranged fee** for the assignment, based on your estimate of how long the work will take; this is quite acceptable, as long as the fee is fair for the work – and the work is fulfilled on that basis.

Contingency fees

Contingency (or percentage) fees depend on the results of the services provided, usually in the form of a percentage of whatever money is gained on behalf of the client.

This is customary where professional help is required to gain the client funds (eg selling an asset or recovering debts). If the assignment is not successful, the client may not be able to pay – and therefore, a percentage fee, contingent on results, is the only way they could gain access to professional services.

Be aware, however, that you *cannot* offer financial reporting services on a contingent fee basis - depending on a specific finding or result being obtained would present a major threat to your professional objectivity!

Expenses

Out-of-pocket expenses that are directly related to the work performed for a particular client (such as travelling expenses) may be charged to the client, for reimbursement, in addition to professional fees.

HOW IT WORKS

You have just had a phone call from a prospective new client, asking about fees. You offer a free-of-charge consultation to discuss the matter. The client has recently left his job to become a freelance photographer; in the first instance, he requires an accountant to prepare financial statements and tax returns, and to advise on financial management.

'How much will you charge per year?' he asks. You explain that your fees are based on an hourly rate, which you quote to him.

'Yes, but how much in total?' he asks. You explain that it will depend on the work involved. You could make an estimate – but you would need authorisation from the partner to whom you report. Moreover, the client would have to be aware that the amount actually billed could be substantially higher, for example, if the client's business arrangements proved to be different from that anticipated.

'Do you reduce the fee if you don't save me as much tax as you thought?' the client asks. You explain that you cannot set a contingent fee on this basis, nor can you make any promises in relation to tax savings. 'What about if I get you to help me with a proposal for an Arts Grant that's available for photographers?' he persists. 'Will you accept a commission on that, instead of an hourly rate?' You agree that this would be possible.

'What about expenses?' pursues the client. 'Will I be paying for all this nice office space?' 'No', you explain. 'This is covered in our overall charge-out rates; you will only be charged out-of-pocket expenses directly related to my work for you.'

Marketing professional services

To attract new clients, accountancy practices must **advertise** their services to the public and businesses. As in any form of advertising there are risks of misrepresenting your services and of making claims that damage the competition, either deliberately or negligently. In other words how a practice advertises itself, and how it tries to win an advantage over its competitors, is an ethical issue.

The AAT Guidelines set out rules on marketing which state:

250.1 When a member in practice solicits new work through **advertising** or other forms of marketing, there may be potential threats to compliance with the fundamental principles. For example, a self-interest threat to compliance with the principle of professional behaviour is created if services, achievements or products are marketed in a way that is inconsistent with that principle.

250.2 A **member** in practice **must not bring the profession into disrepute** when marketing professional services. The member in practice must be honest and truthful and should not:

(i)   make **exaggerated claims** for services offered, qualifications possessed or experience gained or

(ii) make **disparaging references** or unsubstantiated comparisons to the work of another.

If the member in practice is in doubt whether a proposed form of advertising or marketing is appropriate, the member in practice should consult with the AAT.

The general principle is that a professional practice, and its individual members, need to:

- Project an image consistent with the 'dignity' (the high ethical and technical standards) of the profession

- Maintain integrity in all promotional actions and statements

Aggressive following up of contacts and leads is considered good marketing in some contexts – but it can be both counter-productive (by putting clients off) and unethical if you are promoting professional services. If you contact or approach potential clients directly and repeatedly, or otherwise in a 'pushy' manner, you may be open to a complaint of **harassment**.

The content of advertisements

Advertising standards. All advertisements (plus promotional materials, letterheads and other documents issued by the practice) should comply with the law and Codes of Practice with regard to the honesty, truthfulness, clarity, decency and legality of their content.

Fees. If fees are mentioned in promotional material, ensure that the statements are not misleading, e.g. about what is covered and how fees are calculated.

If you use low fees as a promotional tool, make sure that you can provide quality service for that price!

It is not unethical to offer a free consultation, at which fees will be discussed.

Advertising claims. Avoid claims that are subjective, difficult to prove or potentially misleading, particularly with regard to the size of the firm (what does 'the largest' refer to?) or the quality of the firm (can you really prove you're 'the best'?).

Affiliate and student members of the AAT must not specifically mention the AAT when advertising their services.

Competitor comparisons. Be careful if you compare your practice, services or fees to those of others. Such comparisons must be:

- Objective, factual and verifiable
- Relating to the same services (so as not to be misleading)

Disparaging statements. Do not make disparaging references to, or comparisons with, the practice or services of others – even if you think they are justifiable!

Task 5

Advertising low fees to attract new clients is permitted by the AAT Guidelines on Professional Ethics providing they are justified by pointing out that competing firms are over-charging for their services.

	✓
True	
False	

Agency appointments

Clients may ask their accountant to act on their behalf as their agent. This essentially means becoming involved in the affairs of the client, including negotiating and agreeing to contracts with third parties. Any such agreements or contracts made by the agent on behalf of their client (known as the principal) are legally binding on the client, not the agent. In relation to accepting agency appointments the AAT Guidelines state:

251.1 The following guidance refers mainly to **building society agencies** but the principles stated apply also, so far as they are relevant, to other forms of agency.

251.2 The acceptance by a member of any agency may present a threat to **professional independence**. Particular problems occur with building society agencies because of the expansion of their range of services beyond deposit-taking. Members in the UK should note that involvement in any investment activity requires authorisation by the FSA. A member who is not so authorised may act as a bare introducer, that is refer an enquirer to, for example, a list of providers of financial services, provided that the member gives no recommendation of any kind.

251.3 Before accepting an agency from a building society or other body, members should be satisfied:

(i) that their **professional independence** will not be compromised

(ii) that **acceptance will not be rendered inappropriate** by the nature of the services they are to provide or the manner in which those services may be brought to the attention of the public.

The acceptance by a member of any agency may present a threat to professional independence. Members in the UK should note that involvement in any investment activity requires authorisation by the FSA (described in Chapter 1). A member who is not authorised should limit their involvement to simply referring an enquirer to a list of providers of financial services (without giving any recommendations).

Before accepting an agency, members should be satisfied that their professional independence will not be compromised, and that acceptance is appropriate.

Letters of engagement

Once an accountant has accepted an appointment they are required to send an engagement letter to the client which sets out the terms of their agreement.

The AAT Guidelines state:

252.1 Members in practice are expected to agree an **engagement letter** for each client. The purpose of such a letter is to provide written confirmation of the work to be undertaken and the extent of the member's responsibilities.

The following features are recommended for inclusion:

(i) The **nature of the assignment**, the scope of the work to be undertaken and, if appropriate, the format and nature of any report which has to be delivered

(ii) The **timing of the engagement,** that is the date the work is expected to start (and whether such dates are contingent on the provision by the client or others of information), the duration of the work and the dates on which reports are to be made

(iii) Whether the assignment is **monthly**, **annual** or **not recurring** and whether the engagement will continue unless specifically terminated by the client

(iv) The **client's responsibilities**, for example, as to the production of information such as records and books, their format and timing. The client should also be advised that, for example, in relation to tax compliance work a member will only be acting as an agent for the client and that the client is responsible for the tax returns, etc, submitted

(v) That the **responsibility for the detection of irregularities and fraud** rests with the client's management and this would normally be outside the scope of the engagement. Nevertheless it should be made clear, under the terms of the engagement letter, that the client is obliged to provide full information to the member

(vi) The **basis, frequency** and **rate of charge** for services rendered together with the treatment of expenses incurred in connection with the assignment. The incidence of any taxes should also be specified

(vii) The **ownership of books** and **records** created in the engagement and whether the member will exercise a lien over such items if fees remain unpaid or are disputed. The member's policy on retention, destruction and return of records should, if appropriate, be specified

(viii) The **member's actions** on a **fee remaining unpaid** after presentation of the invoice should be dealt with, including the charging of interest and at what rate, the cessation of work and, as above, the exercise of a lien over the client's books and records

(ix) The **usage of the member's work** by the client for third parties should be specified and suitable disclaimers employed

(x) **Liability disclaimer**

(xi) The member's customer **due diligence**, **record-keeping** and **reporting obligations** under the anti-money laundering legislation

(xii) How the member will deal with **commission** or **other benefits** received by the member for introductions to other professionals or suppliers, whether the member's fees will be reduced by amounts received in this connection, and/or whether the member can retain the commission or benefit without having to account to the client.

A **letter of engagement** provides written confirmation of the **agreement** with the client as to the nature and scope of the work to be undertaken, and the responsibilities of both the client and the accountant in the relationship. It is very important in managing client expectations, minimising threats arising from client pressure – and avoiding misunderstandings and later conflicts!

Any time a new assignment is undertaken, or additional tasks are added to an assignment, or the terms of an engagement alter, a new letter of engagement should be submitted. Both parties sign copies of the letter, so that each has a signed agreement for its files.

The following elements are recommended in the AAT Guidelines for inclusion in a standard letter of engagement:

The assignment	The nature of the assignment
	Work to be undertaken (and tasks specifically not included, where relevant)
	Reports to be delivered (scope and format)
Timeframes	Start date (subject to access to information, if relevant)
	Length of the assignment (or date of reporting)
	If the assignment is recurring (eg monthly or annually)
	If the engagement is open-ended (to be terminated by the client)
Client responsibilities	For producing records and books (format, timing)
	For tax returns submitted (since the member is only acting as an agent for the client)
	For provision of full and accurate information
Charges	The basis, frequency and rate of charge for services rendered (including contingency fees if applicable)
	Treatment of expenses
	Billing arrangements

Ownership	Who owns books and records created in the assignment
	The member's policy on retention, destruction and return of records (where relevant)
Unpaid fees	Penalties for non-payment (e.g.: interest charged; cessation of work; and/or the member exercising lien over the client's books and records)
Third parties	Whether the client can share the work with third parties or use it for other purposes
	Disclaimer of liability for other uses

HOW IT WORKS

Catherine, a client with whom your firm has an agreement to provide accountancy services only, has told you that she expects to inherit from a recently deceased uncle. She says she would like your firm to calculate her inheritance tax liabilities with regard to it.

This is not in your original letter of engagement, so you propose that you draw up a new one to cover the task. 'But it will still be included in the fee we agreed, won't it?' the client asks. You answer that the original fee was based on the estimated time it would take to complete the accountancy work. Since you need to ensure that you can give her quality service, you feel that you should negotiate a fee for the additional work.

You draw up a letter of engagement for a non-recurring short-term assignment for the provision of inheritance tax advice. The assignment will be fulfilled by the submission of a letter of advice on the tax implications of her inheritance and for the agreed fee.

Names and letterheads of practices

The requirement to be professionally dignified and not misleading also applies to the practice's **name**, **letter heading** and any **documents** used to communicate with clients and other parties (even the nameplates on the office door!). These matters are also subject to various legal provisions, concerning business names and designations, and the use of partners' and principals' names.

The AAT Guidelines state:

253.1 For the purpose of this section the term **'letterhead'** means any part of the practice's notepaper and documents used by the practice for communicating with clients and other parties and includes advertisements, electronic mail, websites and facsimile material.

253.2 A **practice name** should be consistent with the **dignity of the profession** in the sense that it should not project an image inconsistent with that of a professional practice bound to high ethical and technical standards.

253.3 A **practice name** must **comply with partnership and company law** as appropriate, other laws including those which control rights to use certain names and words and, in the UK with the relevant legislation governing business names.

253.4 A practice name should not be **misleading**, for example:

(i) a practice with a **limited number of offices** should not describe itself as 'international' merely on the grounds that one of them is overseas

(ii) it would be misleading if there was a real risk that the practice name could be **confused with the name of another practice**, even if the member(s) of the practice could lay justifiable claim to the name

(iii) it has been the **custom of the profession** for members to practice under a name based on the names of past or present members of the practice itself or of a practice with which it has merged or amalgamated. A practice name so derived will usually be in conformity with this guidance.

253.5 **Letterheads**, **documents** and other **stationery**, including, so far as applicable, nameplates, used by the practice should meet the following criteria:

(i) they should be of an **acceptable professional standard**

(ii) they must comply with all **legal requirements** including as to names of partners, principals and other participants, and with Article 20(B) of the **AAT's Memorandum and Articles** which **prohibits the use of a member's designatory letters in the name of the practice**

(iii) they should not identify any service provided by the practice as being of a **specialised nature**, unless a member can clearly demonstrate expertise in that particular area.

Task 6

You work for a firm of accountants which has two offices, one based in London and one based in New York. The firm's main competitor has been established longer than your firm and is called Ryland, Fitch, Crombie and Co.

Which of the following names for your firm would be permitted under the AAT's Guidelines on Professional Ethics?

	✓
Luther Crombie and Co	
Fitch and Walker and Co (International)	
Ryland, Fitch and Crombie organisation.	

➡ **Signpost**

See the AAT Guidelines on Professional Ethics:

- **Section 210**: Professional appointment and engagement acceptance
- **Section 220**: Conflicts of interest
- **Section 230**: Second opinions
- **Section 240**: Fees and remuneration
- **Section 250**: Marketing professional services
- **Section 251**: Agency appointments
- **Section 252**: Letters of engagement
- **Section 253**: Names and letterheads of practices

CHAPTER OVERVIEW

- Accounting matters often require the use of **personal judgement** – and opinions as to the best or 'right' way to handle them can sincerely differ. Moreover, people need to develop their own ethical and technical judgement, as part of their own personal and continuing professional development.

- Behaving ethically means acting with integrity, honesty, fairness and sensitivity in dealings with clients, suppliers, colleagues and others.

- Members in business and in practice face numerous **threats** against the AAT's Fundamental Principles. These threats can be classified as self-interest, self-review, familiarity, intimidation and advocacy.

- The AAT's Guidelines on Professional Ethics provide one source of **safeguards** against the threats members face. Other sources of safeguards include the law, corporate governance rules and policies and procedures set out by their employer.

- There are a number of important rules and procedures to follow when a member in practice **acquires new clients**. At all times the law must be followed and respect and dignity should be shown to competitors and the accounting profession. In particular, rules cover:
    - Constraints on the services that can be provided
    - Dealing with conflicts of interest
    - Letters of engagement
    - Transferring clients
    - Money laundering regulations
    - Fees and receiving commission for recommending new clients
    - Giving second opinions
    - Marketing
    - Names and letterheads of practices

TEST YOUR LEARNING

Respond to the following by selecting the appropriate option.

Test 1

The fact that a client employs competent staff with experience and seniority to make managerial decisions can be used as a safeguard against threats to the fundamental principles by an accountant in practice.

	✓
True	
False	

Test 2

If you are acting as an agent for a client, and a third party offers you a gift that might be seen to influence your actions in relation to your principal's business, this may create which types of threat to the fundamental principles?

- Self-interest and intimidation
- Advocacy and self-review
- Familiarity only

Test 3

Which of these represents a threat to professional competence and due care?

- Insufficient or inaccurate information
- A gift from a supplier

Test 4

Which of the following would be included within 'know your client' information in customer due diligence procedures?

- Patterns of business
- Sources of funds
- References
- Identification documents
- Business model

chapter 3:
BEHAVING IN AN ETHICAL MANNER II

chapter coverage 📖

In this chapter, we continue our look at some of the specific situations that may be encountered in public practice or when providing accounting services.

The topics we shall cover are:

✍ Maintaining professional independence

✍ Acting with sufficient expertise

✍ Policies for handling clients' money

✍ Confidentiality and disclosure

✍ Professional liability

✍ Ownership and lien

MAINTAINING PROFESSIONAL INDEPENDENCE

An accountant has a professional duty to maintain an appropriate distance (independence) between their work and their personal life at all times. This is required in order to be able to act objectively, i.e. independence and objectivity are linked. We have already seen the need for independence when we looked specifically at conflicts of interest but the AAT Guidance provides wider rules that you must follow in this regard.

AAT members who work in **practice providing assurance services** need to **maintain independence from their assurance clients**, in order to protect the integrity of their professional services. There is an entire section covering independence with respect to assurance engagements in the AAT Guidelines (section 290). There are two overall requirements:

- **Being independent**. The AAT Guidelines refer to '*independence of mind*" (objectivity) as the ability to put aside all considerations that are not relevant to the decision or task in hand – free from bias, prejudice or partiality.

"The **state of mind** that permits the expression of a conclusion without being affected by influences that compromise **professional judgement**, allowing an individual to act with integrity and exercise objectivity and professional scepticism." (Section 290.8 of the AAT Guidelines).

- **Being seen to be independent** ('*independence in appearance*'): the ability to **demonstrate** independence by avoiding situations that would cause a reasonable and informed observer to question your ability to be objective. Examples include clear **threats to objectivity** such as a personal financial interest in the outcome; a personal relationship with the client; or managerial/operational involvement in activities being reviewed.

"The avoidance of facts and circumstances that are so significant that a **reasonable** and **informed third party**, having knowledge of all relevant information, including safeguards applied, would reasonably conclude a firm's, or a member of the assurance team's, integrity, objectivity or professional scepticism had been compromised." (Section 290.8 of the AAT Guidelines).

Perhaps the most important way of maintaining independence is to be aware that you may be exposed to influences, pressures and other threats to your objectivity.

If you are aware of these pressures, you can analyse them and judge whether there are sufficient **safeguards** in place to reduce the risk of compromise to acceptable levels.

General safeguards include:

- Your own strength of character and professionalism, which enable you to stand up to pressure from a supervisor or client and do the right thing

- Your awareness of your legal accountability, and potential penalties under the law

- Your awareness of your professional accountability, and disciplinary action that may be taken against you by your professional body

- Your awareness of potential negative impact on your professional reputation (and future livelihood)

Task 1

Avoiding situations that would cause a reasonable and informed observer to question your ability to be objective is known as:

	✓
Independence of mind	
Independence in appearance	
Being independent	

We shall now consider some more specific rules on objectivity and independence.

Objectivity and independence – members in practice

The fundamental principle of objectivity requires AAT members who provide assurance services to be independent of their clients. The AAT's Guidelines provide further advice on how members can maintain their objectivity. The Guidelines state:

280.1 A member in practice must consider, when providing any professional service, whether there are threats to compliance with the fundamental principle of objectivity resulting from having **interests in**, or **relationships with,** a **client** or **directors, officers** or **employees** of a **client**. For example, a familiarity threat to objectivity may be created from a close personal or business relationship.

280.2 A member in practice who **provides an assurance service** is required to be **independent of the assurance client**. Independence of mind and in appearance is necessary to enable the member in practice to express a conclusion, and be seen to express a conclusion, without bias, conflict of interest or undue influence of others.

280.3 The existence of threats to objectivity when providing any professional service will depend upon the particular **circumstances of the engagement** and the nature of the work that the member in practice is performing.

280.4 A member in practice must **evaluate** the **significance** of identified **threats** and, if they are not clearly insignificant, safeguards must be considered and applied as necessary to eliminate them or reduce them to an acceptable level. Such safeguards may include:

(i) **withdrawing** from the engagement team

(ii) **supervisory procedures**

(iii) **terminating the financial or business relationship** giving rise to the threat

(iv) **discussing the issue** with higher levels of **management** within the firm

(v) **discussing the issue** with those charged with **governance** of the client.

Objectivity is a vital principle of professional integrity and is particularly important in financial reporting and similar 'assurance services', where independence of mind and in appearance is necessary to enable the member to express a conclusion that is (and can be seen to be) free of bias, conflict of interest or undue influence of others.

The AAT Guidelines state:

290.1 In the case of an **assurance engagement** it is in the public interest and, therefore, required by the fundamental principles set out in these *Guidelines*, that members of assurance teams, firms and, when applicable, network firms be independent of assurance clients.

Before you decide to accept a new appointment or engagement (or to continue with an existing one), you need to consider:

- Potential **threats to objectivity** that may arise – or appear to arise – from the context and/or the people connected with the work.

- What **safeguards** can be put in place to offset the threats – and whether these are sufficient to protect your objectivity (and hence independence).

There are specific situations or threats associated with a lack of professional distance between professional duties and personal life i.e. a lack of independence. These can be relevant to members in business and in practice. We have already considered one such threat – a conflict of interest – in Chapter 2. Now we look at others.

Financial interests (relevant to members in business)

There are a number of ways in which an accountant in business could gain financially from their activities for an employer – and many of these might pose a **self-interest threat** to fundamental ethical principles such as integrity, confidentiality, or objectivity. Other potential threats might be where the accountant, or someone close to the accountant, holds a financial interest (e.g. a loan or shares), is eligible for a profit-related bonus or holds, or is eligible for, share options in the employing organisation. The decisions and reports made or influenced by an accountant may affect the value of such interests (e.g. by inflating profit figures or enhancing share values).

The AAT's Guidelines state:

340.1 Members in business may have **financial interests**, or may know of financial interests of close or personal relations or associates, that could, in certain circumstances, give rise to threats to compliance with the fundamental principles. For example, self-interest threats to objectivity or confidentiality may be created through the existence of the motive and opportunity to manipulate price sensitive information in order to gain financially. Examples of circumstances that may create self-interest threats include, but are not limited to situations where the member in business or close or personal relation or associate:

(i) holds a **direct** or **indirect financial interest** in the employing organisation and the value of that financial interest could be directly affected by decisions made by the member in business

(ii) is **eligible** for a **profit related bonus** and the value of that bonus could be directly affected by decisions made by the member in business

(iii) **holds, directly** or **indirectly, share options** in the employing organisation, the **value** of which could be **directly affected** by decisions made by the member in business

(iv) **holds, directly** or **indirectly, share options** in the employing organisation which are, or will soon be, **eligible for conversion** or

(v) **may qualify for share options** in the employing organisation or performance related bonuses if certain targets are achieved.

340.2 In evaluating the significance of such a threat, and the appropriate safeguards to be applied to eliminate the threat or reduce it to an acceptable level, members in business must examine the nature of the financial interest. This includes an **evaluation** of the **significance of the financial interest** and whether it is direct or indirect. Clearly, what constitutes a significant or valuable stake in an organisation will vary from individual to individual, depending on personal circumstances.

340.3 If threats are not clearly insignificant, safeguards must be considered and applied as necessary to eliminate or reduce them to an acceptable level. Such **safeguard**s may include:

(i) **policies** and **procedures** for a committee independent of management to determine the level or form of remuneration of senior management

(ii) **disclosure** of all **relevant interests**, and of any plans to trade in relevant shares to those charged with the governance of the employing organisation, in accordance with any internal policies

(iii) **consultation**, where appropriate, with **superiors** within the employing organisation

(iv) **consultation**, where appropriate, with those charged with the **governance** of the employing organisation or relevant professional bodies

(v) **internal** and **external audit** procedures

(vi) **up-to-date education** on ethical issues and the legal restrictions and other regulations around potential insider trading.

These rules mean that if significant threats are present (i.e. the interest is direct and of high value), safeguards will have to be put in place. If you think there may be an issue, you should consult with your supervisor, and perhaps with higher authorities. This might include, for example, an independent committee to set remuneration (for senior managers) and the need to disclose relevant interests and share trading to the officials in charge of corporate governance in your organisation.

The bottom line is do not **manipulate** information, and do not **use** confidential information, for your own financial gain.

Gifts, hospitality and inducements

One of the key threats to independence and objectivity (and the appearance of independence and objectivity) is accepting gifts, services, favours or hospitality from parties who may have an interest in the outcome of your work:

- A work colleague (if working in business)

- A client (if working in practice)

- Any party with a current or proposed contractual relationship with your employing organisation: contractors and suppliers for example

These may be (or may be seen as) an attempt to influence the objectivity of your decisions, or to make you do or not do something. You do not personally have to be the intended recipient; gifts to your spouse or dependent children are assumed to be equally compromising.

Note also that if you offer gifts, favours or hospitality, this may be seen as an attempt to unethically influence others.

Does this mean that you cannot accept a bottle of wine at Christmas, or a calendar from a supplier? No. The gift needs to be significant enough that it could be reasonably perceived, by a person who has all the facts, as likely to influence your judgement.

The AAT's Guidelines set out the following rules to members in business and members in practice.

Rules for members in business

The rules on inducements under the AAT's Guidelines state:

350.1 A member in business or their close or personal relation may be offered an inducement. **Inducements** may take various forms, including gifts, hospitality, preferential treatment and inappropriate appeals to friendship or loyalty.

350.2 Offers of inducements may create threats to compliance with the fundamental principles. When a member in business or their close or personal relation is offered an inducement, the situation should be carefully considered. **Self-interest threats** to objectivity or confidentiality are created where an inducement is made in an attempt to unduly influence actions or decisions, encourage illegal or dishonest behaviour or obtain confidential information. **Intimidation threats** to objectivity or confidentiality are created if such an inducement is accepted and it is followed by threats to make that offer public and damage the reputation of either the member in business or their close or personal relation.

350.3 The significance of such threats will depend on the nature, value and intent behind the offer. If a **reasonable** and **informed third party**, having knowledge of all relevant information, would consider the inducement insignificant and not intended to encourage unethical behaviour, then a member in business may conclude that the offer is made in the normal course of business and may generally conclude that there is no significant threat to compliance with the fundamental principles.

350.4 If evaluated threats are not clearly insignificant, **safeguards** must be considered and applied as necessary to eliminate them or reduce them to an acceptable level. When the threats cannot be eliminated or reduced to an acceptable level through the application of safeguards, a member in business should not accept the inducement. As the real or apparent threats to compliance with the fundamental principles do not merely arise from acceptance of an inducement but, sometimes, merely from the fact of the offer having been made, additional safeguards should be adopted. A member in business should assess the risk associated with all such offers and consider whether the following actions should be taken:

(i) where such offers have been made, **immediately inform** higher levels of **management** or those charged with **governance** of the employing organisation

(ii) **inform third parties** of the offer – for example, a professional body or the employer of the individual who made the offer; a member in business should, however, consider seeking legal advice before taking such a step

(iii) **advise close** or **personal relations** or **associates** of relevant threats and safeguards where they are potentially in positions that might result in offers of inducements, for example as a result of their employment situation, and

(iv) inform higher levels of management or those charged with governance of the employing organisation where close or personal relations are employed by **competitors** or **potential suppliers** of that organisation.

The attention of the members serving in UK government, local and public authorities or other public bodies is particularly drawn to the provisions of the **Public Bodies Corrupt Practices Act**, the **Prevention of Corruption Acts** and any other Acts of relevance to public service which remain in force.

Anti-corruption legislation

If you are employed by a public body in the UK (including government and local authorities), the acceptance of gifts may also be illegal under UK anti-corruption legislation (as per s.350.4 of the AAT Guidelines above.

Making offers

350.5 A member in business may be in a situation where the member in business is expected to, or is under other pressure to, **offer inducements** to subordinate the judgement of another individual or organisation, influence a decision-making process or obtain confidential information.

350.6 Such pressure may come from within the **employing organisation**, for example, from a colleague or superior. It may also come from an **external individual** or **organisation** suggesting actions or business decisions that would be advantageous to the employing organisation possibly influencing the member in business improperly.

350.7 A member in business must not offer an inducement to improperly influence the **professional judgement** of a third party.

350.8 Where the pressure to offer an unethical inducement comes from within the employing organisation, the member must follow the principles and guidance regarding ethical **conflict resolution** set out in Part A of these *Guidelines*.

Rules for members in practice

Similar rules apply to members in practice and extracts from the AAT's Guidance are as follows:

260.1 A member in practice, or a close or personal relation, may be offered **gifts and hospitality** from a client. Such an offer ordinarily gives rise to threats to compliance with the fundamental principles. For example, self-interest threats to objectivity may be created if a gift from a client is accepted; intimidation threats to objectivity may result from the possibility of such offers being made public.

260.2 The significance of such threats will depend on the **nature, value** and **intent** behind the offer. Where gifts or hospitality which a reasonable and informed third party, having knowledge of all relevant information, would consider clearly insignificant are made, a member in practice may conclude that the offer is made in the normal course of business without the specific intent to influence decision making or to obtain information. In such cases, the member in practice may generally conclude that there is no significant threat to compliance with the fundamental principles.

260.3 If evaluated threats are not clearly insignificant, **safeguards** must be considered and applied as necessary to eliminate them or reduce them to an acceptable level. When the threats cannot be eliminated or reduced to an acceptable level through the application of safeguards, a member in practice **must not accept** such an offer.

A member in practice who is acting as an **agent**, should also consider potential criminal offences under the Prevention of Corruption Act 1906 and other Acts which may be relevant.

The main points to take from the Guidelines are that inducements are attempts to influence somebody's decisions or actions. These may constitute:

- A **self-interest threat** to integrity, confidentiality or objectivity, if the inducement is made to encourage illegal or dishonest behaviour, to obtain confidential information, or to influence the member's decisions.

- An **intimidation threat** – if an inducement has been accepted, and someone threatens to expose the member (potentially damaging their reputation and career).

Some appropriate safeguards include:

- Informing your boss if an offer (other than something clearly insignificant or customary) has been made

- Informing your boss if a close friend or personal relation of yours is employed by a competitor or potential supplier of your organisation (because an inappropriate appeal to your relationship, friendship or loyalty may be a form of 'inducement')

Task 2

You have been recently employed as a purchases ledger clerk for a construction company. Your manager has been granted ten tickets to attend the Ashes Test Match at Lords Cricket Ground, London, in a corporate hospitality box by a consultancy firm that is bidding for the contract to design your company's new computer system.

This is an ethical issue for you.

	✓
True	
False	

  Signpost

See the AAT Guidelines on Professional Ethics:

- **Section 280:** Maintaining objectivity
- **Section 290:** Maintaining independence (290.1 and 290.8)
- **Section 340:** Financial interests
- **Section 350:** Inducements
- **Section 260:** Gifts and hospitality

HOW IT WORKS

At a training workshop, you are asking other accounts staff to discuss their ethical questions and concerns.

- One accounting technician feels it is dishonest to use work time and systems for personal emails. Another argues that this is part of the 'psychological contract': staff get paid slightly under market rate, so it's understood that small 'perks' can be taken advantage of, as long as the system is not abused. Lively discussion ensues as to where the line is between 'use' and 'abuse'.

- The first speaker accuses the other of dishonesty. You intervene and emphasise that no blame can be attached, since this has been a 'grey area' in the firm. Later, you take the accuser aside privately, and suggest that he gives some thought to the ethics of publicly criticising a professional colleague.

- One sales ledger clerk compares your company's ethics favourably to those of his previous employer, and begins to detail its attempts to infringe copyright. You intervene, and remind him that he owes a duty of confidentiality to his former employer.

- There is some discussion about workplace humour. A cost accountant has been hurt by constant jokes about his religion. The others tell him to 'lighten up' but you draw the group's attention to the laws on religious harassment. The group grows thoughtful…

- Later, one of the staff approaches you and says that he has an ethical dilemma. He exaggerated his past work experience on his CV when applying for the job, and was not questioned on it in the interview. Now, however, he is being given tasks which he is not sure he is competent to perform correctly – but is afraid that if he says anything, he will be accused of getting the job under false pretences, and fired. You advise him to speak honestly with his supervisor – or at least to own up to being 'rusty' in this area: the important thing is not to take on tasks beyond his ability, and to get the help he needs.

We now look at this last issue, of acting with sufficient expertise, in more detail.

ACTING WITH SUFFICIENT EXPERTISE

"The fundamental principle of **professional competence** and **due care** requires that a member in business should only undertake significant tasks for which the member in business has, or can obtain, sufficient specific training or experience. However, if the member in business has **adequate support**, usually in the form of supervision from an individual who has the necessary training and experience, then it may be possible to undertake appropriate significant tasks. A member in business should not intentionally mislead an employer as to the level of expertise or experience possessed, nor should a member in business fail to seek appropriate expert advice and assistance when required." (Section 330.1 of the AAT Guidelines).

A member in business may be asked to undertake a wide range of tasks in the course of your work. Some of these tasks may be significant in their potential impact on the organisation and its stakeholders. And some of them may be tasks for which you have had little or no specific training or direct experience; tasks relating to a specialist field of accountancy, say, or to a specific industry sector or organisation type (such as charities) – or even unfamiliar software and systems.

Potential **threats** to the principle of competence and due care include: time pressure (when there may not be enough time to complete a task properly); insufficient or inaccurate information; lack of resources (e.g. equipment or help); or your own lack of experience, knowledge or training.

These threats may not be significant if you are working as part of a team, or under supervision, or on a comparatively low-level task. If they *are* significant, however, you may need to apply safeguards.

Much as you may enjoy a 'challenge', take great care:

- Not to mislead your employer by stating (or giving the impression) that you have more knowledge, expertise or experience than you actually have!

- To state clearly and assertively that a particular task is outside the boundaries of your professional expertise and experience.

- To be realistic, responsible and proactive in requesting or accessing whatever extra time or resources, advice, help, supervision or training you need to deliver competent performance and to meet agreed deadlines. You may need help from outside the business e.g. from an independent expert or the relevant professional body.

If you cannot get the time, information, resources or help you need to do the job properly, you may have to refuse to do it – explaining your reasons clearly and carefully to your boss.

 Signpost

See the AAT Guidelines on Professional Ethics:

- Section 330: Acting with sufficient expertise

POLICIES FOR HANDLING CLIENTS' MONEY

AAT members who work in practice may come into contact with their clients' money. For example the practice may be involved in paying a client's suppliers or employees. As a consequence it is important that a number of rules and procedures are followed to avoid threats to a number of fundamental principles.

The AAT Guidelines state:

270.1 A member in practice must not assume **custody of client monies** or other assets unless permitted to do so by law and, if so, in compliance with any additional legal duties imposed on a member in practice holding such assets.

270.2 **The holding of client assets creates threats to compliance with the fundamental principles; for example, there is a self-interest threat to professional behaviour and there may be a self interest threat to objectivity arising from holding client assets.** To safeguard against such threats, a member in practice entrusted with money (or other assets) belonging to others should:

(i) **keep such assets separately** from their personal or firm's assets

(ii) **use** such **assets only for the purpose** for which they are **intended**

(iii) at all times, **be ready to account** for those assets, and any income, dividends or gains generated, to any persons entitled to such accounting, and

(iv) **comply with all relevant laws** and **regulations** relevant to the holding of and accounting for such assets. Members operating in the UK cannot hold investment business clients' monies as defined in the relevant UK legislation unless they are regulated by the FSA.

270.3 In addition, members in practice should be aware of threats to compliance with the fundamental principles through association with such assets, for example, if the assets were found to derive from **illegal activities**, such as money laundering. As part of client and engagement acceptance procedures for such services, members in practice should, in appropriate cases, on a risk-sensitive basis, make appropriate inquiries about the source of such assets and should consider their legal and regulatory obligations. They may also consider seeking legal advice.

Handling clients' money – key safeguards

AAT members should remember three issues when handling clients' money, separation, use and accountability.

- **Separation** – clients' monies should be kept separately from monies belonging to the AAT member personally and/or to the practice.

- **Use** – clients' monies should be used only for the purpose for which they are intended.

- **Accountability** – members must be ready at all times to account for the monies to authorised enquirers.

When not to hold clients' monies

As a member in practice you should not hold clients' monies if:

- They are the monies of investment business clients and you are not regulated under relevant authorisation schemes

- There is reason to believe that they are 'criminal property' (obtained from, or to be used for, criminal activities); this would constitute money laundering

Fraud Act 2006

Another area to be aware of when considering the handling of client monies is the penalties for fraud in the event that funds are mishandled. Under the **Fraud Act 2006**, a person is guilty of fraud if they are in breach of any of the following sections of the Act:

- Section 2 (**fraud by false representation**)
- Section 3 (**fraud by failing to disclose information**)
- Section 4 (**fraud by abuse of position**)

It is Section 4 that is most likely to apply to a professional accountant holding client monies, who is tempted to commit fraud. A person is in breach of this section if they:

- Occupy a position in which they are expected to look after the financial interests of another person

- Dishonestly abuse that position and

- Intend, by means of the abuse of that position

  (i)   To make a gain for themselves or another, or
  (ii) To cause loss to another or to expose another to a risk of loss

Any person who is guilty of fraud is liable to a prison sentence or fine.

Task 3

Fill in the missing word below.

Section 4 of the Fraud Act 2006 covers fraud by …… of position.

HOW IT WORKS

Franklin Delaney, your new client, phones to ask if you would hold some money on his behalf, 'for reasons he would rather not discuss at the moment'. Although you have carried out due diligence in confirming Mr Delaney's identity and sources of income, you explain to him that you cannot hold any client's monies without verifying the commercial purpose of the transaction and the source and destination of the funds.

Meanwhile, another client has deposited funds with you, pending completion on a house purchase; the client will be overseas at the time, and you have agreed to liaise with her solicitor to complete the transaction. It is agreed that your own fees may be drawn from the client account.

 Signpost

See the AAT Guidelines on Professional Ethics:

- **Section 270**: Custody of client assets

CONFIDENTIALITY AND DISCLOSURE

As an accountant, you are likely to have access to a great deal of information about the financial affairs of your clients (or your employers and their clients) that would not, in the normal course of business, be disclosed to the public.

All information you receive through your work as an accountant should be regarded as **confidential**: that is, given in trust (or confidence) that it will not be shared or disclosed. Examples include:

- Information shared with the explicit proviso that it be kept **private and confidential**

- Information shared within a **professional/client relationship** (e.g. with an accountant or solicitor), which is regarded as a relationship of 'trust and confidence' under the law

- Information that is **restricted or classified** within an organisation's information system (e.g. marked 'private', 'confidential' or 'for authorised individuals only')

- Information protected by **data protection and personal privacy law** (e.g. in the UK, personal data held by organisations, and personal medical data of employees, covered by the **Data Protection Act 1998**)

- Information that could be used **against the interests** of the organisation or an individual

The Data Protection Act 1998 and the Information Commissioner's Office

The Data Protection Act gives individuals the right to know what information is held about them. It provides a framework to ensure that personal information is handled properly.

Anyone (an individual or a company) who processes personal information (a 'data controller') must comply with eight principles, which make sure that personal information is:

- Fairly and lawfully processed
- Processed for limited purposes
- Adequate, relevant and not excessive
- Accurate and up to date
- Not kept for longer than is necessary
- Processed in line with your rights
- Secure
- Not transferred to other countries without adequate protection

The Act also provides individuals with important rights, including the right to find out what personal information is held about them on computer and most paper records.

Should an individual or organisation feel that they are being denied access to personal information, or that their information has not been handled appropriately, they can contact the Information Commissioner's Office (ICO). The ICO has legal powers to ensure that organisations comply with the requirements of the Data Protection Act.

The Information Commissioner's Office maintains a public register of data controllers. Each register entry includes the name and address of the data controller and a general description of the processing of personal information that is being undertaken. Individuals can consult the register to find out what processing of personal information is being carried out by a particular data controller.

Notification is the process by which a data controller gives the ICO details about the processing of personal information. **Notification is a statutory requirement** and every organisation that processes personal information must notify the ICO unless they are exempt. **Failure to notify is a criminal offence**.

The notification period is one year, and data controllers must re-register. They must also keep the register up to date, so when any part of the entry becomes inaccurate or incomplete, the ICO must be informed within 28 days. Again failure to do so is a criminal offence.

The principal purpose of having notification and the public register is transparency and openness. It is a basic principle of data protection that the public should know (or should be able to find out) who is carrying out the processing of personal information as well as other details about the processing (such as for what reason it is being carried out).

Task 4

Fill in the missing number below.

The Information Commissioner's Office (ICO) maintains a public register of data controllers. If any part of a data controller's register becomes inaccurate then they should notify the ICO within ..... days.

The duty of confidentiality

In Chapter 1 we studied the detailed requirements of the AAT's Guidelines, and we will not repeat them here, but you should remember that they state clearly that:

"...members have an obligation to respect the **confidentiality** of information about a client's or employer's affairs, or the affairs of clients of employers, acquired in the course of professional work."

This may seem obvious, but it extends more widely than you may think:

- It applies even after the assignment, or the contractual relationship with the client or employer is over. In other words, you need to respect the confidentiality of information about former clients and ex-employers too.

- It applies not just to you, but to any staff under your authority, and any people you ask for advice or assistance. It is up to you to ensure that they keep any information you share with them confidential.

When *can* you disclose confidential information?

As we saw in Chapter 1, disclosure of confidential information is a difficult and complex area and members are therefore specifically advised to seek professional advice before disclosing it.

You are permitted to disclose confidential information in three specific sets of circumstances (see section 140.7 of the AAT Guidelines):

(1) **When you are properly authorised to do so**

The client or employer may legitimately authorise you to disclose the information. However, you still need to consider the effect of disclosure; will it be in the best interests of all the parties involved in the matter?

(2) **When you have a professional duty to do so**

You are entitled to disclose information if it is necessary to do so in order to perform your work properly, according to the technical standards and ethical requirements of the profession.

You also have a duty to disclose information if asked to do so by the AAT or another regulatory body, as part of an ethical or disciplinary investigation into your conduct (or the conduct of your employer or client).

(3) **When you have a legal duty to do so**

UK law requires you to:

(a) Produce documents or give evidence if asked to do so by a court of law, in the course of **legal proceedings** against you, or your client or employer.

(b) Disclose certain information to bodies that have **statutory powers** to demand the information, such as **HM Revenue and Customs**.

(c) Disclose certain **illegal activities** to appropriate public authorities. Not all illegal activities must be reported in this way; there may be other regulatory machinery for dealing with them. However, some activities are covered by specific legal provisions, particularly in relation to public safety, organised crime, money laundering and terrorism.

HOW IT WORKS

Your in-tray this morning contains three requests for information:

- You receive a formal demand from HM Revenue and Customs for information regarding the VAT returns of a client.

  You report this to one of the partners, who says he will refer the matter to the firm's legal advisers.

- A property developer, who is a client of yours, has written asking whether you know of any businesses in the city looking to sell a commercial property.

  You recall that a petrol station client of yours has told you that they are intending to sell. However, you are also aware that the value of the property (for its current purposes) will fall once a scheme for a new by-pass is announced. Both these facts are covered by client confidentiality.

  You call the petrol station owners and ask them if you can disclose their plans to the property developer. They give permission, so you pass the message to the developer. At the same time, you advise him of the need to carry out 'due diligence' for any purchase, including checking any development applications already under consideration by the Town Planners – without suggesting any specific reason to do so. You follow up with a letter to both the petrol station owners and the property developers, recommending that they seek independent advice regarding the sale/purchase; this enables you to avoid taking on a conflict of interest between the two clients (if one wins and one loses from the transaction).

- A new employee has given you her banking details, for payroll. She has also included some information about the rates of pay and benefits paid by her previous employer, and some of its payroll practices – apparently just to explain how delighted she is by the generosity and integrity of your company.

  This data may have been given in good faith – but it is inappropriate to disclose confidential details of a previous employer. You delete the e-mail, having recorded the relevant banking details. You also make a note to have a quiet word with her about confidentiality.

Factors to consider in disclosing information

Even if the information can legitimately be disclosed, you still have to consider a number of points in deciding whether or how to proceed:

- **How reliable is the information?** If all the relevant facts are known and supported by good evidence, the disclosure may be clear cut – but if all you have is unsupported facts, opinions or suspicions, you may have to use your professional judgement as to whether you disclose, how and to whom.

- **Who is the appropriate recipient of the information?** You need to be sure that the person to whom you give the information is the right person; in other words, they have a legitimate right to it, and the authority to act on it.

- **Will you incur legal liability by disclosing the information?** Some disclosures (such as reporting money laundering) are legally 'privileged' and you cannot be sued for breach of professional confidentiality. This is as long as the disclosure is made in good faith and with reasonable grounds. Other situations may not be so clear cut and you may need to consider getting advice from a solicitor before proceeding with a disclosure without the client's authorisation.

- **How can you protect the on-going confidentiality of the information as far as possible?** If you make a disclosure, you have a responsibility to ensure that it is made only to the relevant parties, and that they understand their responsibilities to protect the information from further disclosure. At least, ensure that you send the information direct to the relevant party, clearly labelled 'confidential' or 'for your eyes only'.

In Chapter 4, we will look at the specific case of disclosure of information by an employee of illegal or unethical practices by his or her employer – this is known as whistleblowing.

PROFESSIONAL LIABILITY

Members may be liable (open to legal action and payment of damages) on a number of grounds: criminal acts, breaches of trust, breaches of contract or statutory liability (e.g. for workplace accidents). However, the AAT Guidelines only deal specifically with liability for members in practice arising from **professional negligence**, in section 257:

257.1 Members may incur legal liabilities in respect of their professional work in a number of different ways, for example, for **negligence**, **breach of contract**, **criminal acts**, **breaches of trust** or under various statutes. The following guidance is concerned only with liability for professional negligence including negligent performance of contractual terms.

In their professional work, members owe their clients (and sometimes other third parties) a duty to exercise **reasonable care and skill**. If members (or their employees or business partners) breach this duty, they may be liable for losses which are caused (which could be substantial). Because of the need to keep the ethical guidelines to reasonable proportions, it is only possible to give some summary guidance here. A member who has any doubt about the extent of his or her liabilities when entering into contracts with clients, or generally, is recommended to seek legal advice. Although the guidance which follows is framed in terms of UK law, similar considerations are likely to apply in most legal regimes.

257.2 Before carrying out any work for a client a member should ensure that the exact duties to be performed and in particular any significant matters to be excluded have been agreed with the client in writing by a **letter of engagement** or otherwise. If the member is asked to perform any additional duties at a later date these should also be defined in writing.

257.3 In giving **informal advice** at the request of a client, or advice which must necessarily be based on incomplete information, a member should make it clear that such advice is subject to limitations and that consideration in depth may lead to a revision of the advice given.

257.4 When **publishing documents** generally, a member may find it advantageous to include in the document a clause disclaiming liability. Such a clause cannot however be relied on in all circumstances. For example, a court might hold that such a disclaimer represented an unreasonable exclusion of liability.

257.5 When submitting **un-audited accounts** or **financial statements** to the client, a member should ensure that any special purpose for which the documents have been prepared is recorded on their face and in appropriate cases should introduce a clause recording that the document is confidential and has been prepared solely for the private use of the client.

257.6 When giving a reference to a third party with regard to **future transactions** (for example, payment of rent) a member should state that it is given without financial responsibility on the part of the member.

257.7 Where the circumstances appear to warrant it because of the complexity of an assignment or otherwise a member should either **seek specialist advice** or suggest that the client should do so.

257.8 The attention of all members in practice is drawn to the need to maintain an adequate level of **Professional Indemnity Insurance** cover in accordance with the Scheme for Members in Practice. Professional Indemnity Insurance is strongly recommended for student members who undertake self-employed work.

The effect of these guidelines are that you have a contractual **duty of care** to your clients: a duty to carry out your professional work with due skill, care, efficiency and timeliness, with proper regard for the technical and professional standards expected of you. Lack of understanding or knowledge on your part is not a legitimate excuse (or legal defence) for giving a client incorrect advice!

If you – or an employee or associate – do something (or fail to do something) that results in financial loss to a person to whom a duty of care is owed, you may incur liability for professional negligence. This can result in claims for substantial damages.

Documents often include a clause **disclaiming liability** (along the lines of: 'No responsibility can be accepted for …'). This may provide extra transparency for clients as to the need to exercise caution in relying on advice, but it cannot be relied on as a legal protection from liability; courts may regard them as an attempt to wriggle out of legitimate responsibility.

Basic safeguards are as follows:

Step 1   Ensure that the exact scope of your duties (what specific matters are included and not included) is set out in your contract or letter of engagement to the client.

Step 2   If any additional duties or services are undertaken at a later date, ensure that these, too, are defined in writing.

Step 3   Ensure that the client is aware of the limitations and constraints that affect your advice (especially if the advice requested is informal or based on incomplete information).

The same applies to unaudited accounts or financial statements submitted to clients. These should clearly state that they are confidential, unaudited and prepared solely for the private use of the client.

Step 4   Disclaim liability where it is legitimate to do so.

Step 5   Ensure that you have adequate Professional Indemnity Insurance to cover your potential liability (as set out in the scheme for self-employed members).

Step 6   If an assignment presents particularly complex or heavy liability issues, seek specialist legal advice – or advise the client to do so.

Task 5

The AAT's Guidelines on Professional Ethics provide rules to help protect members from professional liability claims in respect of:

	✓
Health and safety legislation	
Professional negligence	
Criminal actions	

HOW IT WORKS

A short while ago, you were asked by an estate agent to provide a financial reference for a client who was looking to enter into a rental agreement. Having checked with the client, you drafted the reference and sent it to your manager for approval. He has now sent back an amended copy, asking you to add the following items:

- The enclosed reference has been prepared without an audit

- The enclosed reference has been prepared from information, records and explanations supplied by the client

- The firm disclaims all financial responsibility for the reference, or for decisions taken in relying upon the information provided

 Signpost

See the AAT Guidelines on Professional Ethics:

- **Section 257**: Professional liability of members

OWNERSHIP AND LIEN

Ownership of books and records

Accountants in practice base much of their work on the books and records provided by their clients and during the working process they generate working papers and files which document what was done. It is important to be aware of who owns the documents in the event of any dispute (for example regarding payment) that may occur. This is because very often the accountant will look to hold onto all the files until their bill has been paid by the client.

The AAT Guidelines state:

254.1 The rules concerning the **ownership of books** and **records** as between a client and a professional person engaged by the client to perform agreed services derive, in the UK, mainly from a combination of statute law and case law. The following paragraphs summarise the principal points on which members may require guidance. It is however stressed that, before entering into contracts with clients, all members should inform themselves of the local legal position and take steps to ensure that the engagement letter covers, as far as reasonably possible, the respective rights and responsibilities.

254.2 Where particular documents and records are not owned by the member they **generally belong to the client**. In determining whether documents and records belong to the member the following considerations apply:

(i)   the **nature of the contract** between the member and the client usually as evidenced in an engagement letter

(ii) the **capacity** in which the member acts in relation to the client

(iii) the **purpose** for which the documents and records exist or are brought into being

(iv) **local law**.

254.3 As a general rule, under UK law, where the member is acting as a principal (and not as an agent) in relation to the client, only documents brought into being by the member on the specific instructions of the client belong to the client. Documents prepared, acquired or brought into being by the member, solely for the member's own purpose as a principal, **belong to the member**. At times however the member may be acting as an agent for a client in which case any documents will generally be the property of the client.

254.4 In audit assignments, for example all documents prepared by the auditor solely for the **purpose of carrying out the audit** belong under UK law to the auditor. Whilst our members may be involved in audit work, they are reminded that they are not permitted to act as auditors for limited companies or charities unless appropriately registered to do so, in the case of the UK, with the appropriate recognised professional body.

254.5 In accountancy work the question of ownership will depend on the **nature of the work**. Accounting records and financial statements prepared for a client belong, under UK law to the client. A member's working papers belong to the member.

254.6 In **taxation work**, the documents will normally belong to the client.

254.7 Where tax, investment or other advice is given to a client, the **written advice**, including supporting papers, belongs, under UK law, to the client, but a member's working papers belong to the member.

254.8 **Letters** received by the member from the client, copies of letters from the member to the client and notes made by the member of discussions with the client belong, under UK law, to the member.

254.9 Ownership of **copies of communications** between the member and third parties depends on the relationship with the client. If the member is acting as agent for the client (for example, in tax correspondence) letters to the member and copies of the member's letters to the third party belong, under UK law to the client. However, where the member acts as principal, the communications will belong to the member.

The ownership of books and records is mainly determined by **law** (check the position in your own country, if not the UK), but specific rights and responsibilities may also be as agreed in the **contract** (or letter of engagement) between the parties.

In common law, ownership also depends on the **capacity** in which you act for the client:

- If you are acting as a **principal** (and not as an agent) for the client, documents and records prepared, acquired or created by you, for your own purposes, belong to you. Only documents that have been created by you on the specific instructions of the client belong to the client.

- If you are acting as an **agent** for the client, documents will generally belong to the client.

In accounting work, the **purpose** of the documents and records is also relevant:

- Accounting records and financial statements prepared for a client belong to the client. Your working papers belong to you.

- In taxation work, documents normally belong to the client.

- Written advice and supporting papers (on tax, investment or other matters) given to a client belong to the client – but your working papers belong to you.

- Letters that you receive from the client, copies of letters you send to the client, and your notes on discussions with the client all belong to you.

- Letters exchanged with third parties belong to you if you are acting as principal – and to the client if you are acting as his or her agent.

Lien

As we saw above, an accountant may seek to hold onto the client's documents until their fees have been paid. This is because once the service has been provided what can the accountant do to enforce payment apart from refusing to return the client's property?

In legal terms an accountant has a right (or lien) to hold onto documents that were used in performing the services until the fees are paid. We shall look at the legal side of things shortly, but for now we shall consider the AAT's Guidelines on the matter.

The AAT Guidelines state:

255.1 When a member has, in the UK, carried out work on the documents of a client and the bill the member has rendered has not been paid, the member will have, under UK law, what is called a **particular lien** over those documents. This means that the member will be able to retain possession of the documents until his or her fees have been paid for the work carried out in relation to those documents.

255.2 The member will have a **right of lien** where all three of the following conditions exist:

(i) the documents retained are the **property of the client** and not of a third party

(ii) the documents have come into the **member's possession** by **proper means**, and

(iii) **work has been done by the member on the documents**, the member has rendered an adequately detailed fee note and **the fees are outstanding** in respect of that work. For example, a member is not able to exercise a lien in respect of documents of the same client on which past, remunerated work was carried out or where fees are outstanding on the part of a company, but the work was carried out on documents which are the personal property of a director. Further, special rules apply in relation to the statutory books and accounting records of companies, and where documents are claimed by an Administrator or Liquidator of a company, or the Official Receiver or a Trustee in Bankruptcy. Further guidance can be obtained from the AAT's Professional Standards team or from a solicitor.

In legal terms, this means where you have carried out work on client documents and presented your bill, but the bill has not been paid, UK law gives you the right to retain possession of the documents until your fees have been paid. (This is called a '**particular lien**' over the documents.)

You have a **right of lien** if:

- The documents belong to the client (not a third party) *and*

- The documents have legitimately come into your possession (e.g. have not been obtained under false pretences) *and*

- You have worked on the documents and tendered a fee note – but the fees have not been paid in respect of *that particular work*.

You cannot exercise lien in relation to the statutory books and accounting records of companies, or where documents are claimed by an Administrator, Liquidator, Official Receiver or Trustee in Bankruptcy; they have a prior claim to the documents.

Retention of documents

Accountants should keep hold of certain documents (such as taxation records and working papers) just in case they need to be referred to in future. For example, a client may be investigated by the tax authorities and your records are needed to show how their tax payments were calculated. However, there is the possibility that clients may attempt to sue the accountant because they believe they received negligent advice. In this instance the working papers may prove that the accountant acted properly.

The AAT Guidelines relating to the retention of documents state:

256.1 The following paragraphs summarise the general position in the UK regarding the **retention of books**, **working papers** and **similar documents**.

256.2 There is a general principle that, after the passage of a given period of time, an action may not be brought before the courts. The law requires that persons with a legitimate cause should make their claim within a reasonable time.

256.3 A number of statutes lay down specific periods of time within which actions must be commenced. However, where statutes do not specify time limits, the **Limitation Act of 1980** and any successor legislation, sets out the general position on time limits. The current position is:

(i) **twelve years** for actions upon a **specialty** (a contract under seal or an obligation under seal securing a debt) or a judgement given by the courts

(ii) **six years for actions based upon a simple contract or tort**, or three years from the earliest date on which the plaintiff or any person in whom the cause of action was vested before that person first had both the knowledge required for bringing an action for damages in respect of the relevant damage (including any claim based on fraud or where the cause of action has been deliberately concealed) and a right to bring such action subject to a maximum period of fifteen years. The result of this is that members should retain books, working papers and other documents for the period of limitation, i.e. no less than six years. Since a disaffected client or other person could issue a writ against the firm before the end of the expiry of the six year period, and delay serving it for up to a year, seven years might, in fact, be the most prudent retention period.

256.4 **Taxation records** should be retained **for 7 years**.

256.5 Members should note that there may be significant differences between UK law and the law of **other countries** where the time limits quoted above will not necessarily apply.

256.6 Members who are in **doubt** about the time limits applicable to the retention of books, working papers or other documents should **consult their legal advisers**.

As a general principle, the '**statute of limitations**' means that once a certain amount of time has passed since a particular act or event, a legal action cannot be brought in relation to that act or event. Specific time limits apply for different matters (and in different legal systems), so you will need to get legal advice in detailed cases.

However, in the UK the time limit is six years for actions based on a simple contract or claim for civil damages. Six years is therefore the maximum time before which a disgruntled client could bring legal proceedings against the firm. Allowing another year to have it brought to court, **seven years** is probably the most sensible period to retain (and advise clients to retain) books, **working papers** and other documents.

Taxation records should be retained for **seven years**.

Task 6

Fill in the missing number below.

In the UK claims against an accountant in respect of a simple contract must be brought within ..... years.

 Signpost

See the AAT Guidelines on Professional Ethics:

- **Section 254**: Ownership of books and records
- **Section 255**: Lien
- **Section 256**: Retention of books, working papers and other documents

CHAPTER OVERVIEW

- An accountant has a professional duty to maintain an **appropriate distance** (independence) between their work and their personal life at all times

- There is a self-interest threat if members in business, or their close or personal relations or associates have **a financial interest** in their employing organisation.

- Gifts and hospitality (in the case of members in practice) or inducements (to members in business) can also pose self-interest and intimidation threats to an accountant's integrity, confidentiality and objectivity.

- Potential threats to the principle of **competence and due care** include: time pressure (when there may not be enough time to complete a task properly); insufficient or inaccurate information; lack of resources (eg equipment or help); or your own lack of experience, knowledge or training.

- Key principles in handling or **holding clients' monies** are separation, dedicated use and accountability.

- Under the **Fraud Act 2006**, a person is guilty of fraud if he or she is in breach of its Sections 2–4

- All information you receive through your work as an accountant should be regarded as **confidential**

- The **Data Protection Act** gives individuals the right to know what information is held about them. It provides a framework to ensure that personal information is handled properly

- **Data controllers** must register with the Information Commissioner's Office each year

- You are permitted to disclose confidential information in three specific sets of circumstances: when you are properly **authorised** to do so; when you have a **professional** duty to do so; when you have a **legal** duty to do so

- If you do something (or fail to do something) that results in financial loss to a person to whom you owe a duty of care, you may incur liability for **professional negligence**

- The ownership of **books and records** depends on legal provisions, contract terms, the capacity in which you act for the client and the purpose of documents and records

- You may retain possession of documents (exercise a **right of lien**) in pursuit of unpaid fees in relation to those documents

- Documents should be retained for at least the **period of limitation**, during which a legal action may be brought

TEST YOUR LEARNING

Respond to the following by selecting the appropriate option.

Test 1

What is the main principle to be remembered when considering conflicts of interest?

- The interests of one client must not have a negative effect on the interests of another

- Adverse disclosures or reports about one client will always benefit another

- You should never take on an assignment where a conflict of interest is present

Test 2

When you have a conflict of interest, it is enough to disclose that information to the parties involved.

- True
- False

Test 3

How long should books, working papers and other documents be retained?

- Six years
- Seven years
- Ten years

Test 4

Clients' monies should be kept separately from monies belonging to you personally, or the practice. How can this be achieved?

- Keeping the money as cash
- Keeping each client's money in a separate account
- Using a different bank

Test 5

You will always have a right of lien over client records if your fees have not been paid.

- True
- False

chapter 4:
TAKING APPROPRIATE ACTION

chapter coverage 📖

Unfortunately, ethical issues are seldom clear-cut. You may often encounter situations where a course of action appears to be on the 'borderline' between ethical (or at least widely accepted) and unethical.

How do you know which is the 'right' course of action in a given situation or interaction? This chapter offers some guidance.

The topics we cover are:

✍ Identifying appropriate ethical behaviours

✍ Taxation services

✍ Money laundering

✍ Conflicting loyalties

✍ Dealing with ethical conflicts

✍ Dealing with illegal or unethical conduct by an employer

IDENTIFYING APPROPRIATE ETHICAL BEHAVIOURS

Ethics and the law

To be ethical, conduct must also be legal. You need to comply with the law, encourage your colleagues and employers (where relevant) to comply with the law – and advise your clients to comply with the law.

You may have encountered a range of legal issues in your personal life or workplace; be aware that these are all potentially relevant to professional ethics, insofar as they affect your behaviour and reputation as an accounting technician!

Task 1

Give five examples of laws that affect (or should affect) your everyday behaviour at work – not necessarily in the way you perform your accounting duties.

Critical decision-making on ethical issues

When considering what to do about an ethical issue, first of all, consider the application of available **legal** and **ethical guidelines** in the particular situation you are facing:

- How might the principles apply?
- Are there examples (or legal precedents) that might act as a template?

If the situation is still unclear, critical decision-making may be required. Two sets of ideas may be useful in helping you to reach a reasoned conclusion that will withstand later scrutiny:

- **Consider the consequences**. What will be the effects of the course of action – on you and others? An action may have both positive and negative impacts, or may affect some people positively and others negatively. However, a course of action that is likely to have an unacceptably high cost for any of the parties concerned may be said to be unethical.

   A basic test is to consider whether you would feel comfortable and confident, if you had to defend your decision or action before a court, or in the press, or to a moral/spiritual adviser you admire? If not, this may be an indication that, deep down, you know that it is potentially unethical.

- **Consider your obligations**. What do you 'owe' other people in the situation? Some obligations are clearly set out in contracts (e.g. with employers and clients) – but we also, arguably, have a general 'duty' to treat others fairly and humanely.

  A basic test (using the 'golden rule', which is part of all major ethical systems) is to consider: would you want to be on the receiving end of whatever action you are about to take? If not, this may be an indication that it is potentially unethical.

So the key questions are:

  (a) Is it legal and in line with company policy and professional guidelines?

  (b) How will it make me feel about myself?

  (c) Is it balanced and fair to all concerned?

There are also outside sources of advice and guidance, which you may choose to access – but it is important to observe the requirement for **confidentiality** until you are sure that the situation is such that you have a right and duty to disclose it.

Getting help with ethical concerns and dilemmas

If you are employed by an organisation, any matter of ethical concern – whether or not it is explicitly addressed in the AAT's Guidelines – should be raised with your immediate supervisor, if possible.

However, if the ethical issue concerns the organisation, or if you are self-employed, you may need to seek independent advice – within the requirements for professional confidentiality:

- Seek **independent legal advice** (particularly if there are potential legal consequences to your actions). Legal advisers are also bound by professional confidentiality, so this offers protection to you and the others involved in the situation. (Talking to a spouse, friend or colleague does not!)

- If you are still in doubt about the proper course of action, you can contact the **AAT's Ethics Advice line** (e-mail: ethics@aat.org.uk), presenting all the relevant facts.

Written records should be kept of any such discussions and meetings (as for other forms of conflict resolution at work), to ensure that there is evidence of the advice you have received. This will help protect you in any legal proceedings that may result.

HOW IT WORKS

At your firm of Chartered Accountants, you have been asked by the partner to whom you report to sit in and take notes as she interviews an applicant for the post of receptionist with the firm.

In the course of the interview, your attention is drawn to the following aspects of the discussion:

- The partner, having learned that the candidate has three small children, asks lots of questions about her plans to have more children and her childcare arrangements. When the candidate, in return, asks about the firm's family-friendly working policies, you notice that the partner omits to mention the childcare assistance that you know is available.

- The candidate reveals that the family depends mainly on income from her husband's job at a local electrical goods manufacturer. As it happens, this company is one of your clients – and you are aware of its plans to shut down the local plant over the coming year.

- The candidate left her previous employers because they continued to employ a successful member of their sales staff who had sexually harassed her and another female employee. This firm is another client of your firm.

After the candidate has left, the partner looks across at you and rolls her eyes and says: 'Just lose those notes, will you?'

What are the ethical issues raised here, and how will you decide what (if anything) to do about them?

- The partner's focus on family responsibilities may be construed as sexual discrimination under UK law – unless she asks the same questions of any men she interviews for the job.

- Giving incomplete information about the organisation might be more significantly unethical if its effect was to mislead someone into taking employment under false pretences. In this case, not much harm is being done, as the candidate is merely being influenced against accepting a job that she probably will not be offered.

- You may feel sorry for the family, who are unaware that the husband will soon lose his job. But this is a fact of economic life – and you have the overriding duty not to disclose what you know about the client's plans.

- The behaviour of the candidate's previous employer is unethical. But you have come by the information indirectly – and is it anything to do with you? It would certainly be in your client's best interests not to risk legal claims against them.

- The partner's request to you to 'lose the notes' is ambiguous. It sounds unethical – whether as a suggestion of prejudice against the candidate, or as a way of dodging responsibility for the ethical issues raised.

So what might you do? First you might decide to clarify exactly what the partner meant; this would clear up any misunderstanding, and highlight the ethical issues more clearly. It might also be possible to draw her attention (respectfully) to the risks of her interview questions being construed as discrimination.

Other than this, it may not be your place to do much more – although you may choose to advise your clients of the ethical and legal considerations that have come to your attention: the need to be socially responsible in notifying employees as early as possible of impending redundancies; and the need for consistency, fairness and compliance with regard to disciplinary issues (such as sexual harassment).

TAXATION SERVICES

Much of the work firms of accountants do for individuals and companies concerns the preparation of tax returns and supplying tax advice. This can present the accountant with ethical dilemmas because clients want to minimise the amount of tax they pay, but the law requires the accountant to ensure they do not break the law.

The AAT Guidelines state:

160.4 A member providing professional **tax services** has a duty to put forward the best position in favour of a client or an employer. However, the service must be carried out with professional competence, must not in any way impair integrity or objectivity and must be consistent with the law.

160.5 A member should not hold out to a client or an employer the assurance that any tax return prepared and tax advice offered are **beyond challenge**. Instead the member should ensure that the client or the employer is aware of the limitations attaching to tax advice and services so that they do not misinterpret an expression of opinion as an assertion of fact.

160.6 A member should only undertake taxation work on the basis of **full disclosure by the client** or **employer**. The member, in dealing with the tax authorities, must act in good faith and exercise care in relation to facts or information presented on behalf of the client or employer. It will normally be assumed that facts and information on which business tax computations are based were provided by the client or employer as the taxpayer, and the latter bears ultimate responsibility for the accuracy of the facts, information and tax computations. The member should avoid assuming responsibility for the accuracy of facts, etc. outside his or her own knowledge.

160.7 When a member **submits a tax return** or **tax computation** for a taxpayer client or employer, the **member is acting as an agent.** The nature and responsibilities of the member's duties should be made clear to the client or employer, in the case of the former by an engagement letter

160.8 **Tax advice** or opinions of material consequence given to a client or an employer **should be recorded**, either in the form of a letter or in a memorandum for the files.

160.9 A **member should not be associated with any return or communication** in which there is reason to believe that it:

(i)   contains a **false** or **misleading statement**

(ii) contains **statements** or **information furnished recklessly** or without any real knowledge of whether they are true or false or

(iii) **omits** or **obscures information** required to be submitted and such omission or obscurity would mislead the tax authorities.

160.10 In the case of a member in practice, acting for a client, the **member should furnish copies of all tax computations to the client** before submitting them to HMRC.

160.11 When a member learns of a **material error** or omission in a tax return of a prior year, or of a failure to file a required tax return, the **member has a responsibility to advise promptly the client or employer of the error or omission and recommend that disclosure be made to HMRC.** If the client or employer, after having had a reasonable time to reflect, does not correct the error, the member should inform the client or employer in writing that it is not possible for the member to act for them in connection with that return or other related information submitted to the authorities. Funds dishonestly retained after discovery of an error or omission become criminal property and their retention amounts to money laundering by the client or employer. It is also a criminal offence in the UK for a person, including an accountant, to become concerned in an arrangement which he knows or suspects facilitates (by whatever means) the acquisition, retention, use or control of criminal property by or on behalf of another person. Other EU states have equivalent provisions. In each of these situations, the member must comply with the duty to report the client's or employer's activities to the relevant authority, as explained in the following paragraph.

160.12

(i)   A member in practice whose **client refuses to make disclosure** of an error or omission to HMRC, after having had notice of it and a reasonable time to reflect, is obliged to report the client's refusal and the facts surrounding it to the MLRO if the member is within a firm, or to the appropriate authority (SOCA in the UK) if the member is a sole practitioner. The member must not disclose to the client or any one else that such a report has been made if the member knows or suspects that to do so would be likely to prejudice any investigation which might be conducted following the report.

(ii) An **employed member in business** whose employer refuses to make disclosure of an error or omission to HMRC:

(a) where the employed member in business has acted in relation to the error or omission, he or she should **report the employer's refusal** and the surrounding facts, including the extent of the member's involvement, **to the appropriate authority** as soon as possible, as this may provide the member with a defence to the offence of facilitating the retention of criminal property

(b) where the employed member in business has not acted in relation to the error or omission, he or she is not obliged to report the matter to the authorities. However, if the member does make a report to the appropriate authority, such will not amount to a breach of the member's duty of **confidentiality**

(iii) Where a member in business is a contractor who is a 'relevant person' for the purposes of the **Money Laundering Regulations 2007** in the UK or equivalent legislation in another EU State or other overseas jurisdictions, the member should act in accordance with Paragraph 160.12(i) above, as though he were a member in practice. However, where the member in business is not a such relevant person, he should act in accordance with Paragraph 160.12(ii) above.

All members have a responsibility to make themselves familiar with anti-money laundering and terrorist financing legislation and any guidance issued by the AAT in this regard.

160.13 The **tax authorities in many countries have extensive powers** to obtain information. Members confronted by the exercise of these powers by the authorities should seek appropriate legal advice.

Tax errors and omissions are specifically mentioned in the guidance notes for the syllabus. Particular ethical issues are raised by performing taxation services (preparing tax returns, giving tax advice and so on), since there is a complex administrative and legal framework for both direct taxation (based on income, gains, profits and losses) and indirect taxation (such as Value Added Tax).

The **AAT's sponsoring bodies** that deal with taxation (ICAEW, ICAS, CIMA and CIPFA – see Chapter 1), and the **Chartered Institute of Taxation**, have extensive ethical guidelines in this area – and the AAT's own Guidelines recommend that UK members seek advice from the Director of Professional Development where required.

Key issues are **integrity**, **technical competence** and **confidentiality**. The following general principles, covered in the Guidelines, apply to both direct and indirect taxation.

Task 2

What should you do if a client asks you how much tax you will be able to save them this year?

	✓
Provide them with a reasonable estimate based on what you achieved last year.	
Tell them that you will save them as much as possible.	
Tell them that you cannot provide such information.	

Ethical reporting

- You have a duty to **put forward the best position**, in favour of your employer or client. However, you need to ensure that you do this with integrity (not falsifying the position), objectivity (on the basis of the facts), professional competence (in line with technical standards and procedures) and compliance (in line with the law).

- You have a duty towards the tax authorities to **provide information in good faith**. You should only undertake tax work on the understanding that your client or employer will make full and accurate disclosure of the relevant information. While you need to exercise reasonable care in accepting and presenting information on their behalf, it is the taxpayer (the client or employer) who bears ultimate responsibility for the accuracy of the data and computations; do not take on responsibility for the accuracy or completeness of information that is outside your own knowledge.

- Do not associate yourself with a tax return or related communication if you have any reason to believe that it is **false** or **misleading**, eg:

  - If it contains a false or misleading statement

  - If it leaves out or obscures information that should be submitted, in such a way as to mislead the tax authorities

  - If it contains statements or information that have been provided carelessly, without the taxpayer checking or knowing whether they are true or false (and therefore being potentially false or misleading)

What if you become aware of errors or omissions?

- If you become aware of a significant error or omission in a tax return from a previous year, or of a failure to file a required tax return, you must immediately advise your client or employer – and recommend that they inform HMRC. (It is not normally your duty to make the disclosure, and you should not do so without the permission of the client or employer, as a confidentiality issue.)

- If an employer or client refuses to correct the problem, you should inform them that you cannot act for them with regard to that return or communication. If you are a self-employed practitioner, you should cease to act for the client, and inform them in writing. You should also inform HMRC that you have ceased to act for that client – adding (where relevant, and only if you yourself were acting for the client with regard to the error or omission) that you have received information indicating that the accounts or statements should not be relied upon.

The **HM Revenue and Customs** authorities have extensive legal powers to obtain information that may otherwise be withheld. If a statutory demand for information is made, you should seek legal advice.

You should also note that for the purposes of the money laundering provisions, the proceeds of deliberate tax evasion – including under-declaring income and over-claiming expenses – are just as much 'criminal property' as money from drug trafficking, terrorist activity or theft. You therefore have a duty to report the client's or employer's activities to the relevant authority (such as the MLRO).

Task 3

What should you do if you become aware of a significant error in a tax return that you prepared and submitted for a client in a previous year?

	✓
Do nothing as admitting errors will damage your professional reputation.	
Correct the error by adjusting this year's tax return to compensate.	
Tell the client to advise HMRC about the error.	

HOW IT WORKS

You have been thinking over some misgivings that you have over one of your clients, a catering business. While you have been able to ensure that personal expenditures of the owners have not been included in the accounts of the business, you have not had a satisfactory response with regard to some concerns that you have regarding undeclared income in its office catering arm.

The owners supply you with a general assurance, in writing, that all income is being declared. However, you have lingering doubts. The business is not reducing its purchases of supplies, nor the hours of its delivery staff – yet recorded sales are still very low when compared with comparable periods in previous years. At the same time, you note that mobile phone costs of all staff are being claimed as business expenses, on the grounds of 'extensive off-site trading'.

It is now time to prepare the client's tax return.

Having discussed the matter with one of the partners, you meet with the client to ensure that they understand that they are responsible for making full and accurate disclosure to the tax authorities, and are prepared to sign a statement to this effect. They reply that, as they see it, you are supposed to be 'on their side' to save them tax. You explain your professional and legal obligations and emphasise that you cannot knowingly associate yourself with a misleading return. As long as you have reason to believe that there may be errors or omissions, you will not be able to act for them in preparing or submitting this return.

 Signpost

See the AAT Guidelines on Professional Ethics:

- **Section 160**: Taxation services

MONEY LAUNDERING

A key example of the need to take appropriate action over illegal or unethical activities is the case of **money laundering**.

According to the **CCAB Anti-Money Laundering Guidance for the Accountancy Sector**:

"In UK law money laundering is defined very widely, and includes all forms of handling or possessing criminal property, including possessing the proceeds of one's own crime, and facilitating any handling or possession of criminal property. Criminal property may take any form, including in money or money's worth, securities, tangible property and intangible property. Money laundering can be carried out in respect of the proceeds of conduct that is an offence in the UK as well as most conduct occurring elsewhere that would have been an offence if it had taken place in the UK. For the purpose of this Guidance, money laundering is also taken to encompass activities relating to terrorist financing, including handling or possessing funds to be used for terrorist purposes as well proceeds from terrorism. Terrorism is taken to be the use or threat of action designed to influence government, or to intimidate any section of the public, or to advance a political, religious or ideological cause where the action would involve violence, threats to health and safety, damage to property or disruption of electronic systems. Materiality or de minimis exceptions are not available in relation to either money laundering or terrorist financing offences."

There can be no hard and fast rules on how to recognise it, but money laundering is generally defined as **the process by which the proceeds of crime, and the true ownership of those proceeds, are changed so that the proceeds appear to come from a legitimate source.** In UK law, it is an offence to obtain, conceal or invest funds or property, if you know or suspect that they are the proceeds of criminal conduct or terrorist funding ('criminal property'). The maximum period of imprisonment that can be imposed on a person found guilty of money laundering is 14 years. An unlimited fine may also be imposed.

You may think that you are unlikely to come across criminal property – but it is not all about the kinds of crime you see on TV cop shows! It includes the proceeds of tax evasion, benefits obtained through bribery and corruption, and benefits (e.g. saved costs) arising from a failure to comply with a regulatory requirement (e.g. cutting corners on health and safety provisions). Even small amounts are included in the definition.

Financial institutions and non-financial businesses and professions are required to adopt specific measures to help identify and prevent money laundering and terrorist financing, including:

- Implementing client checking, record-keeping and internal suspicion-reporting measures. This includes the appointment of a **Money Laundering Reporting Officer (MLRO)**.

- Not doing or disclosing anything that might prejudice an investigation into such activities. This specifically includes any word or action that might '**tip off**' the money launderers that they are, or may come, under investigation. You are, however, entitled to advise clients on issues regarding prevention of money laundering on a non-specific basis.

- **Disclosing** any knowledge or suspicion of money laundering activity to the appropriate authorities. It is specifically stated that accounting professionals will not be in breach of their professional duty of confidence (and therefore cannot be sued) if they report, in good faith, any knowledge or suspicions in relation to money laundering, to the appropriate authority.

Proceeds of Crime Act 2002

The **Proceeds of Crime Act 2002 (POCA)** created a single set of money laundering offences applicable throughout the UK to the proceeds of all crimes. It also created a disclosure regime, which makes it an offence not to disclose knowledge or suspicion of money laundering. The definition of money laundering offences in POCA includes even passive possession of criminal property as money laundering.

POCA established a number of money laundering offences including:

- Principal **money laundering** offences

- Offences of **failing to report** suspected money laundering

- Offences of **tipping off** about a money laundering disclosure, tipping off about a money laundering investigation and **prejudicing** money laundering investigations

Under POCA there is a duty to report knowledge or suspicion about money laundering – this is referred to in POCA as 'authorised' or 'protected' disclosures. The difference between the disclosures is that an '**authorised**' disclosure is made by the money launderer themselves – '**protected**' disclosures are made by someone who knows or suspects another of money laundering.

CCAB Anti-Money Laundering Guidance for the Accountancy Sector

The composition of the Consultative Committee of Accountancy Bodies (CCAB) was described in Chapter 1. It has published its own anti-money laundering guidance with reference to the **Proceeds of Crime Act 2002** (POCA) and the **Money Laundering Regulations 2003 and 2007**.

There is no minimum ('de minimis') amount to be taken into account when any suspicion of possible money laundering offences arises. In other words, 'criminal property' is never identified by its value. A person commits a money laundering offence when:

- Criminal property is concealed, disguised, converted, transferred or removed

  An arrangement is made which facilitates the acquisition, retention, use or control of criminal property

- Criminal property has been acquired or used (except where adequate consideration was given)

Failing to disclose, tipping off and prejudicing an investigation

Failure to make a disclosure in the form of a '**suspicious activity report**' (SAR) to SOCA, or an **internal report** to an MLRO, is an offence. This is accompanied by the offences of 'tipping off' and 'prejudicing an investigation'.

'**Tipping off**' amounts to alerting someone either that a disclosure about suspected money laundering has been made, or that an investigation is being contemplated or carried out. The offence of '**prejudicing an investigation**' occurs when a person knows that a money laundering investigation is being conducted and makes a disclosure to that effect (thereby hampering investigation efforts) or falsifies or destroys documents relevant to the investigation.

Required disclosure

The obligation to make the required disclosure arises when:

- A person knows or suspects (or has reasonable grounds for doing so) that another person is engaged in money laundering

- The information on which the knowledge or suspicion is based arose in the course of business in the regulated sector

- The suspect can be identified, or there is information which can assist with identification and which can help concerning the whereabouts of the laundered property

A person commits an offence if he fails to disclose this knowledge or suspicion, or reasonable grounds for suspicion, as soon as practicable to a nominated officer or SOCA.

The following information forms part of the required disclosure

- Identity of the suspect (if known)
- The information on which the knowledge or suspicion is based
- Whereabouts of the laundered property (if known)

 Signpost

The AAT has issued separate guidance on money laundering, available from its website: www.aat.org.uk. You should be aware that detailed guidance exists, if you encounter a situation in which you think it might be relevant.

HOW IT WORKS

When you visited your client's café business recently, you noticed that they had employed an additional chef – but now, checking the payroll reports, you cannot find any mention of this person, or any payments made to her.

You need to check that your suspicions (that the employee is being paid cash to avoid tax liabilities) are well-founded, but you are aware of the danger of '**tipping off**' the client. Payroll fraud is an offence, reportable to the SOCA (or Money Laundering Reporting Officer in your firm); if you prepare financial statements covering it up, you are party to the concealment of 'criminal property'.

Your first step is to discuss the matter with one of the partners. He advises you to speak to the client in general terms about the seriousness of accurate and truthful reporting. If the situation does not then change (and the payroll 'omission' is not put right), your firm's MLRO will be consulted.

Task 4

Fill in the missing number below.

The maximum penalty for being found guilty of money laundering is ...... years in prison.

CONFLICTING LOYALTIES

If you are an employed member of a professional body, or a 'member in business', you owe a **duty of loyalty** to your employer and to your profession. The AAT Guidelines state clearly that: 'A member in business has a responsibility to further the legitimate aims of their employing organisation. [Professional ethical codes] do not seek to hinder a member in business from fulfilling that responsibility, but consider circumstances in which conflicts may be created with the duty to comply with the fundamental principles'.

Where does your duty lie?

As an employee, your first duty will generally be to contribute to your organisation's objectives (ends), and to comply with all reasonable instructions, requests, rules and procedures (means) designed to further them. But what if some of these ends or means are unethical (as defined by the standards of your profession)? Where does your primary duty lie?

Your employer cannot legitimately require you to:

- Break the law
- Break the rules and standards of the accounting profession
- Put your name to, or otherwise be associated with, a statement which significantly misrepresents facts (particularly in connection with financial statements, tax or legal compliance)
- Lie to or mislead regulators or the firm's internal or external auditors
- Facilitate, or be part of, the handling of unethical or illegal earnings (i.e. Money Laundering)

The law and rules and standards of your profession take clear priority in such a conflict of loyalties: your duty is to refuse to obey the instruction or rule, unless it can be shown that it is not, after all, incompatible with legal and professional requirements.

This may be easier said than done, particularly if you are a junior employee and are being put under pressure by an influential (or personally overbearing) superior. You may need all your assertive communication techniques!

At the same time, it is worth remembering that not every difference of opinion on ethical issues is an ethical conflict – and not every ethical conflict is significant enough to present a real conflict of loyalties. In other words, pick your battles wisely!

DEALING WITH ETHICAL CONFLICTS

The AAT Guidelines set out some advice to members concerning how ethical conflicts should be dealt with:

310.1 A **member in business has a professional obligation to comply with the fundamental principles**. There may be times, however, when their responsibilities to an employing organisation and the professional obligations to comply with the fundamental principles are in conflict. Ordinarily, a member in business should support the legitimate and ethical objectives established by the employer and the rules and procedures drawn up in support of those objectives. Nevertheless, where compliance with the fundamental principles is threatened, a member in business must consider a response to the circumstances.

310.2 As a consequence of responsibilities to an employing organisation, a member in business may be **under pressure** to act or behave in ways that could directly or indirectly threaten compliance with the fundamental principles. Such pressure may be explicit or implicit; it may come from a supervisor, manager, director or another individual within the employing organisation. A member in business may face pressure to:

(i) **act contrary** to **law** or **regulation**

(ii) **act contrary to technical** or **professional standards**

(iii) be a **party** to or facilitate management strategies for **unethical** or **illegal earnings**

(iv) lie to, or otherwise **intentionally mislead** (including misleading by remaining silent) others, in particular:

    (a) the **internal** or **external auditors** of the employing organisation

    (b) **regulators**

(v) issue, or otherwise be associated with, a financial or non-financial report that **materially misrepresents the facts**, including statements in connection with, for example:

    (a) the **financial statements**

    (b) **tax compliance**

    (c) **legal compliance**

    (d) **reports** required by **securities regulators**.

310.3. The significance of threats arising from such pressures, such as intimidation threats, must be evaluated and, if they are not clearly insignificant, **safeguards** must be considered and applied as necessary to eliminate them or reduce them to an acceptable level. Such safeguards may include:

(i) **obtaining advice** where appropriate from within the employing organisation, an independent professional advisor or a relevant professional body

(ii) the existence of a **formal dispute resolution process** within the employing organisation

(iii) seeking **legal advice**.

What is an ethical conflict?

It is almost inevitable that at some time in your career, you will meet a situation that presents some kind of ethical dilemma or conflict, where:

- Two ethical **values or requirements** seem to be incompatible, e.g. you have the duty to disclose unethical conduct that has come to your attention – but also the duty of professional confidentiality.

- Two sets of **demands and obligations** seem to be incompatible ('conflicting loyalties'), e.g. if an employer or client asks you to break the ethical guidelines of your profession: falsifying a record; making a misleading statement; or supplying information 'recklessly', without being in a position to know whether or not it is true.

  Such situations may be particularly acute if you are put under pressure to do the wrong thing by an overbearing supervisor, or by a valued client, friend or relation.

Note that not everyone thinks alike on all ethical matters! It is quite possible that a fellow professional, or a work colleague, will honestly disagree with you about what constitutes an ethical or unethical course of action; this does not necessarily mean that you have an 'ethical conflict', or that you have to report and formally resolve the matter!

The kind of genuine ethical conflict that must be resolved is one that puts you in a position where you are being asked or required to take – or be party to – action that you feel may be unethical.

Resolving ethical conflicts

The AAT Guidelines provide a structure for resolving ethical conflicts as follows:

100.16 In evaluating compliance with the fundamental principles, a member may be required to **resolve a conflict** in the application of fundamental principles.

100.17 When initiating either a **formal** or **informal conflict resolution process**, a member should consider the following, either individually or together with others, as part of the resolution process:

(i) **relevant facts**

(ii) **ethical issues** involved

(iii) **fundamental principles** related to the matter in question

(iv) **established internal procedures** and **alternative courses of action**.

Having considered these issues, a member should **determine the appropriate course of action that is consistent with the fundamental principles** identified. The member should also weigh the consequences of each possible course of action. If the matter remains unresolved, the member should consult with other appropriate persons within the firm or employing organisation for help in obtaining resolution.

100.18 Where a matter involves a conflict with, or within, an organisation, a member should also consider consulting with those charged with **governance of the organisation**, such as the board of directors or the audit committee.

100.19 It may be in the best interests of the member to **document the substance of the issue** and details of any discussions held or decisions taken, concerning that issue.

100.20 If a significant conflict cannot be resolved, a member may wish to **obtain professional advice** from the relevant professional body or legal advisors on a confidential basis and thereby obtain guidance on ethical issues without breaching confidentiality. For example, a member may suspect that he has encountered a fraud and may need to discuss confidential information in order to satisfy himself whether his suspicions are justified. In such circumstances, the member should also consider the requirement under the anti-money laundering legislation to submit a report to SOCA or to the firm's Money Laundering Reporting Officer (MLRO)

100.21 If, after exhausting all relevant possibilities, the ethical conflict remains unresolved, a member should, where possible, **refuse to remain associated with the matter creating the conflict**. The member may determine that, in the circumstances, it is appropriate to withdraw from the engagement team or specific assignment, or to resign altogether from the engagement, the firm or the employing organisation.

If you are asked, instructed or encouraged to take a course of action that is illegal, or unethical by the standards of your profession, you are entitled and required to refuse.

This can lead to interpersonal – and perhaps even legal – conflict.

Some issues may be 'cleared up' by **informal discussion**; they may be based on a misunderstanding, or ignorance – or the belief that no-one knows what is going on! Your first aim will be to persuade the relevant parties not to take (or persist in) the unethical course of action.

If informal discussion does not work, and the issue is significant, more formal avenues may be pursued.

Within an organisation (for members in business), there may be **established procedures** for resolving ethical issues and conflicts with colleagues or superiors, such as those for dealing with grievances. If this does not produce a satisfactory result, the problem should be discussed with the next level up in the management hierarchy, and/or arbitrators such as an Ethics Committee or those in charge of corporate governance (eg the board of directors or audit committee). If a conflict still exists after all internal avenues to resolution have been explored, the accountant may have no alternative but to resign.

Similarly, in a self-employed situation (for members in practice), if a client requests or instructs you to take a course of action that is unethical or illegal, you are entitled and required to refuse. The request may be made in ignorance and good faith – and you should attempt to explain the technical, legal and ethical principles that apply. If the client continues to insist, or refuses to change his or her own unethical conduct (where this reflects on you as his or her agent or adviser), you should simply cease to act for that client.

If the issue is unresolved, even if you have taken steps to protect your own integrity and reputation by resigning or ceasing to act, you may still have a duty to report illegal or unethical conduct to relevant authorities. This is a tricky area, because of the competing duty of confidentiality.

HOW IT WORKS

You have some concerns regarding inaccuracies in the amounts of time some of your colleagues charge their clients which often result in clients paying for an accountant's time which has not been spent on the client's work. When you report this to the partner she says 'Forget it, the clients are still getting good value for money one way or another. Do you think the partners waste time tying down every hour that goes astray here or there? You worry too much.'

There will be an ethical conflict if you choose to pursue the matter (as compromising your professional ethics) and the partner insists that you let the matter drop. The culture of your firm, from the top down, is clearly unsympathetic to what are seen as 'minor' ethical concerns. You may have to go to the Ethics Committee (which should include impartial members), or get independent advice (from the AAT or a legal adviser) as to whether or how to take the matter further.

Meanwhile, you have sat in on another interview for the post of receptionist. This candidate, who is very keen and is currently working for another firm of chartered accountants in the city, appears to be the perfect person for the job. As the partner is bringing the interview to a close, the candidate says: 'By the way, I thought you might like to see the kind of systems I've got experience with. Here's a copy, on disk, of our Contacts Management software.'

After the interview, you tell the partner that you are not comfortable about this. She says that although it is, technically, a breach of copyright, she will destroy the disk after looking over it; this is probably within the definition of 'fair dealing'.

You suspect, however, that the candidate has actually handed her a competing firm's (highly confidential) client/contact list. This would clearly be unethical to accept, let alone use. Does the partner have similar suspicions, or is she acting in ignorance? Did the candidate offer the disk in good faith – or as an incentive to influence the selection decision? You should state your concerns clearly about this. If the partner knowingly takes advantage of unethically-obtained information, and expects you to be silent about it, you are being made party to an unethical course of action; this is a serious ethical conflict, and you should get confidential independent advice on how to deal with it.

 Signpost

See the AAT Guidelines on Professional Ethics:

- **Section 100**: Ethical conflict resolution (100.16 – 100.21)

DEALING WITH ILLEGAL OR UNETHICAL CONDUCT BY AN EMPLOYER

In addition to ethical conflicts directly affecting your own work, you may become aware that your employers have committed (or may be about to commit) an act that you believe to be illegal or unethical.

Examples include:

- Various forms of **fraud**

- **Falsification of records**, or the supply of information or statements that are false or misleading

- The **offer of inducements** to influence external parties (such as government officials) who have power to help or hinder the employer's operations. This may take the form of bribes (payments made to secure services to which a company is not legally entitled) or 'grease money' (payments made to speed up services that are being stalled or obstructed). 'Gifts' are more problematical (particularly in some cultures, where they are regarded as part of civilised negotiation), but they are unethical if their intent is to influence decisions in the company's favour (e.g. to win a contract).

- The **acceptance of inducements** to help or hinder the interests of others, or to compromise objectivity and impartiality. For example, clients may offer inducements to collude in fraud or money-laundering, to overlook financial irregularities and so on.

- Other **illegal activity** – from health and safety violations, to money-laundering, to breach of copyright, sexual discrimination or misuse of personal data.

Your aim in dealing with such a situation is, initially, to persuade your employer not to initiate or complete the act, or to put things right and/or to change its policies and controls to ensure that the problem does not occur again. There may be specific machinery to facilitate this process, or you may have to report the matter to successive levels of management with the power of decision-making in relevant areas.

There may be an Ethics Committee in the organisation: a group of executives (perhaps including non-executive directors) appointed to oversee company ethics and to make rulings on allegations of misconduct.

HOW IT WORKS

A payroll clerk at your company approaches you and asks if you can give her some personal advice. You say that you will try to help – if you can – on the understanding that you cannot take responsibility.

It appears that the production department has been tipped off that a Health and Safety Inspector will be visiting the factory in a couple of days, following a complaint. Apparently, the factory supervisors are busy replacing safety guards on machinery, and covering up torn flooring – and generally disguising potential safety hazards. Now the production manager has asked the payroll clerk for a management report on sickness and injury pay, but the specific parameters he has set for the information will make it look as if there have been fewer and less serious accidents than has in fact been the case.

At this point, you stop the clerk and say that it would be inappropriate for you to hear more, but in your opinion this may be a genuine ethical conflict (if all the facts are true), as she is apparently being asked knowingly to present a misleading report. You advise her to speak in the first instance to her own supervisor, stating her concerns and asking the supervisor to take the matter up with the production manager.

Whistle blowing

Whistle blowing is the disclosure by an employee of illegal or unethical practices by his or her employer. Theoretically, this ought to be welcomed as in the public interest – but remember: confidentiality is also a very strong value in the accountant's code of ethics.

This is an important issue, because:

(a) You are in a position to uncover information that you may feel requires disclosure.

(b) You may be the one who is given information by a concerned employee or whistleblower.

The Public Interest Disclosure Act

The Nolan Committee on Standards in Public Life made the following comments on 'whistleblowing':

"All organisations face the risk of things going wrong or of unknowingly harbouring malpractice ... Encouraging a culture of openness within an organisation will help: prevention is better than cure. Yet it is striking that in the few cases where things have gone badly wrong in local public spending bodies, it has frequently been the tip-off to the press or the local MP ... which has prompted the regulators into action. Placing staff in a position where they feel driven to approach the media to ventilate concerns is unsatisfactory both for the staff member and the organisation."

In the UK, the **Public Interest Disclosure Act 1998** is part of employment legislation and offers some protection to employees in the private, public and voluntary sectors, ensuring that they cannot suffer detriment for disclosing otherwise confidential information, or to an appropriate regulator, if they do so in good faith and have reasonable grounds to believe:

- That **civil, criminal, regulatory or administrative law** is being breached or is likely to be breached

- That the **health or safety** of any individual has been, is being or is likely to be endangered

- That the **environment** has been, is being or is likely to be damaged and/or

- That **information** on any of the above has been, is being or is likely to be deliberately concealed

The background to the Act was a spate of scandals and disasters in the 1980s and 1990s in the UK, where almost every public enquiry found that workers had been aware of dangers but had either been too scared to raise the alarm, or had raised the matter in the wrong way or with the wrong person.

The Act sets out the circumstances where the disclosure of malpractice outside the organisation is in the public interest and should be protected. The question of whether particular information may, regardless of confidentiality, lawfully be disclosed in the public interest will always need to be carefully considered.

For a disclosure to be protected:

(a) The whistleblower must make the disclosure honestly

(b) For external disclosures, there must be a substantive basis for the belief that there is malpractice

(c) For wider public disclosures, the concern should be raised internally first

Where a whistleblower is victimised or dismissed, he can bring a claim for damages to an employment tribunal.

Confidentiality or 'gagging' clauses in employment contracts and severance agreements (that stop an employee from speaking out) are void if they conflict with the protection given by the Act.

The most ethical approach may be to encourage and use available lines of communication within the company – so that there is less need to whistleblow externally.

Task 5

If you begin to suspect that your manager is using his position in your organisation to launder money, who should you report this to?

	✔
SOCA	
The Police	
Your firm's MLRO (providing they are not your manager)	

 Signpost

See the AAT's separate guidance notes:

- *The ethics of whistle blowing*

Downloadable from the AAT website: www.aat.org.uk.

 Signpost

See the AAT Guidelines on Professional Ethics:

- **Section 300**: Threats and safeguards applying to members in business
- **Section 310**: Potential ethical conflicts and dilemmas

CHAPTER OVERVIEW

- Generally speaking, ethical conduct is **legal conduct**

- When making an ethical decision, it can help to (i) consider the **consequences** and (ii) consider your own **obligations**

- A **basic test** is to consider whether you want to be on the receiving end of whatever action you are about to take

- If you are employed by an organisation, any matter of ethical concern should be raised with your **immediate supervisor**. If you are self-employed, you may need to seek **independent advice**

- The **AAT's Ethics Advice Line** is also available

- Particular ethical issues are raised by performing **taxation services**. When you submit a tax return or computations for a client or employer, you are acting as an agent of the taxpayer

- You have a **duty** to put forward the best position, in favour of your employer or client. You also have a duty towards the tax authorities to provide information in good faith

- As an accountant you are required to be vigilant for instances of **money laundering** – the attempt to conceal the identity of money created as a consequence of illegal activities

- In any **conflict of loyalties**, the requirements of the law and your professional standards take precedence – although you should use your judgement as to whether they will be seriously compromised enough to take action through grievance or ethics procedures

- **Not everyone thinks alike on ethical matters**; it is quite possible that a colleague will honestly disagree with you about what constitutes an ethical or unethical course of action

- If you are asked, instructed or encouraged to take a course of action that is illegal, or unethical by the standards of your profession, you are **entitled and required to refuse**

- If you suspect that your employers have committed or may commit an illegal or significant unethical act, your first aim is to persuade them to stop or to put the matter right. If they do not, you may have to make a **disclosure** to an appropriate regulator – but you should seek **independent legal advice**

- **Whistle blowing** is the disclosure by an employee of illegal or unethical practices by his or her employer. Employees are protected from victimisation by the **Public Interest Disclosure Act**

TEST YOUR LEARNING

Respond to the following by selecting the appropriate option.

Test 1

A self-employed AAT member with an ethical dilemma should seek advice from:

	✓
An independent legal expert or an employee with ethics training	
The AAT Ethics Advice line or a close friend	
An independent legal expert or the AAT Ethics Advice line	

Test 2

You have a duty towards the tax authorities to

	✓
Provide information in good faith	
Put forward the best possible position for the client on the basis of the information they provide you	

Test 3

The HM Revenue and Customs authorities have extensive legal power to:

	✓
Compel an accountant to cease to act for a client	
Prosecute a tax agent for failing to get the best possible refund for his or her client	
Obtain information that may otherwise be withheld	

Test 4

If you are an employed member of a professional body you owe a duty of loyalty to

	✓
The AAT and HMRC	
Your employer and your client	
Your employer and your profession	

Test 5

In a self-employed situation, if a client requests or instructs you to take a course of action that is unethical or illegal, you are entitled and required in the first instance to

	✓
Terminate the appointment at once	
Refuse	
Report your client to the relevant authorities	

Test 6

The Public Interest Disclosure Act 1998

	✓
Protects employees from being dismissed for public disclosures if they act in good faith	
Ensures that employees who whistleblow will be dismissed if they act outside the public interest	
Protects employees from suffering detriment for internal whistleblowing, or reporting to a regulator, in good faith	

ANSWERS TO CHAPTER TASKS

CHAPTER 1 – The principles of ethical working

1   This is personal to you, so that you begin to think about your own assumptions and beliefs about what kinds of behaviour are 'OK' and 'not OK'. Some of these may be in line with the ethical values of the AAT and accounting profession (such as being honest, telling the truth, being fair and working hard) and some may not be (such as using your work position for the benefit of family members, or offering gifts as a smoother of business relationships and negotiations). In a way, these instances – where your values differ from the professional standards – are more useful information: you know where your 'blind spots' are, and where you may have to modify your assumptions and habits.

2   False. Straightforwardness and honesty are related to the fundamental principle of integrity.

3   Maintain. Accountancy professionals attain competence by passing professional exams and gaining relevant experience. It is the *maintenance* of professional competence that requires continuing awareness and understanding of relevant technical, professional and business developments and is achieved through CPD.

4   If they are asked for during legal proceedings.

    In this case you have a legal duty to disclose the information.

5   'Significant pressure' indicates intimidation threat.

6   The Professional Oversight Board (POB) acts as an independent body responsible for monitoring the regulation of the accountancy profession by the professional accountancy bodies.

7   Openness is a principle identified by the Nolan Committee.

8   Damage to assets is a loss which results from physical risk.

9   False. The AAT's guidelines do not have the force of law.

CHAPTER 2 – Behaving in an ethical manner I

1   The examples you come up with will be relevant to you or your work. However, some examples of common dishonest behaviour include:

- Stealing property

- Using company information for person gain

- Knowingly selling products with defects

- Damage to physical assets – vandalism

- Using pirated software

- Deliberately producing inaccurate or misleading information

2   Self-review threat.

According to the AAT's Guidelines on Professional Ethics, a member of an assurance (audit) team who has recently been an officer or director of the client is an example of a self-review threat.

3   Whether acceptance would create any threats to compliance with the fundamental principles.

Whilst the client's profitability and ethical standards may be considered by the firm, the AAT's Guidelines do not require them to be considered.

4   True.

The situation might arise where the accountant has to act for one of the clients to the detriment of the other.

5   False.

Low fees are permitted providing a quality service can be provided at that price. However the statement goes on to make a disparaging remark about the competition which is contrary to the AAT's Guidelines on Professional Ethics.

6   Luther Crombie and Co.

This name is unlikely to be confused with the competing firm (unlike Ryland, Fitch and Crombie) and does not portray itself to be an international firm (as Fitch and Walker and Co (International) does).

CHAPTER 3 – Behaving in an ethical manner II

1   Independence in appearance

Avoiding situations that would cause a reasonable and informed observer to question your ability to be objective is known as independence in appearance.

2   False

Whether it is an ethical issue depends on a number of factors, such as:

- The value of the hospitality: a sporting event would not normally be regarded as significant – but it would depend on how lavish the package was (or how rare the tickets).

- The circumstances: in this case, the fact that the host is bidding for a major contract might suggest an attempt to influence the decision.

In this case, there is probably no ethical issue for you as you are not the one with the authority to make the decision.

However, due to the value of the event and the circumstances, it is likely to be an issue for your manager.

3   Abuse.

4   28 days.

5   The AAT's Guidelines on Professional Ethics provide rules to help members avoid actions against them for professional negligence.

6   6 years.

CHAPTER 4 – Taking appropriate action

1   Examples include: health and safety at work; data protection (use of data held by organisations about individuals); equal opportunity and non-discrimination (including avoiding offensive and harassing behaviour towards others on grounds of sex, race and religious beliefs); and company law (e.g. on retention of documents). Plus – of course – not committing common law offences such as theft, fraud or assault!

2   Tell them that you cannot provide such information.

   You should not make any statement or promises in this regard, since you are not realistically in a position to do so.

3   Tell the client to advise HMRC about the error.

   Since you acted for the client with regard to the faulty return, you should advise the client to inform HMRC.

4   The maximum penalty for being found guilty of money laundering is 14 years in prison.

5   Your firm's MLRO (providing they are not your manager).

   The guidelines on what to do about this are set out in law and regulations in the UK. In this case, you have a clear duty to 'blow the whistle' to the appropriate internal authority (the Money Laundering Reporting Officer).

TEST YOUR LEARNING – ANSWERS

CHAPTER 1 – The principles of ethical working

1. False. Group values are very important: eg in families and friendship groups (which is where we get our ideas from), national cultures and organisations (which establish ethical norms and expectations by which we have to operate).

2. Enhance the reputation and standing of its members (so that, for example, they are able to attract and retain clients).

3. A personal financial interest in the client's affairs will affect objectivity. Failure to keep up to date on CPD is an issue of professional *competence*, while providing inaccurate information reflects upon professional *integrity*.

4. This is an issue of technical competence and due care. You should clarify the limits of your expertise with the client, and *then* seek information or guidance from the relevant source.

5. The basic procedure is:

    - Identify a potential threat to a fundamental ethical principle

    - Evaluate the seriousness of the threat

    - Apply safeguards to eliminate or reduce the threat to an acceptable level

    - Discontinue the action or relationship giving rise to the threat (only if the threat cannot be eliminated or reduced to an acceptable level).

6. It is in the public interest that services are carried out to professional standards.

7. - Accounting Standards Board
    - Financial Reporting Review Panel
    - Professional Oversight Board
    - Auditing Practices Board
    - Accountancy and Actuarial Discipline Board

8   External events. These events might fall under one of the headings: internal fraud; external fraud; employment practices and workplace safety; clients, products and business practice; damage to physical assets; business disruption and systems failures; processes and delivery of outputs.

9   ▪ Selflessness
     ▪ Honesty
     ▪ Objectivity
     ▪ Accountability
     ▪ Leadership

The remaining principles, not on this list, are 'integrity' and 'openness'.

10   False. Any fine will be limited to a maximum figure set by the AAT Council.

CHAPTER 2 – Behaving in an ethical manner I

1   True.

Reliance on safeguards built into a client's system (such as employing competent staff) can be used by an accountant in practice as a safeguard against threats to the fundamental principles. AAT Guidelines on Professional Ethics (200.17).

2   Self-interest and intimidation.

The self-interest threat is created as you now have an interest in the transaction. There may also be intimidation against you once you have accepted the gift if its purpose is dubious. This is because the person providing the gift may threaten to expose your acceptance unless you do as they say.

3   Insufficient or inaccurate information. You must be prepared to state when you feel uncomfortable with a particular task due to lack of experience or proper resources.

4   Patterns of business; sources of funds; business model. Sufficient knowledge of a client must be maintained to enable you to identify unusual transactions.

CHAPTER 3 – Behaving in an ethical manner II

1   **The interests of one client must not have a negative effect on the interests of another**. It is often impossible to act in the best interests of both clients at the same time.

2   **False**. The clients must then decide if they are happy for you to continue to act for them.

3   **Seven years**. In the UK, the time limit is six years for actions based on a contract or a claim for civil damages. Six years is therefore the maximum time before which a client could bring legal proceedings, so it is sensible to keep records for a further year to allow time for any action to come to court.

4   **Keeping each client's money in a separate account**; It is not necessary to use a different bank and keeping the money as cash makes no difference,

5   **False**. For example, you cannot claim a lien in relation to the statutory books and accounting records of companies, or over documents that are owned by a third party.

CHAPTER 4 – Taking appropriate action

1   **An independent legal expert or the AAT Ethics Advice line**. Employees or close friends should not be asked due to confidentiality issues.

2   **Provide information in good faith**. You should only undertake tax work on the understanding that your client or employer will make full and accurate disclosure of the relevant information.

3   **Obtain information that may otherwise be withheld**

4   **Your employer and your profession**. The AAT Guidelines state: 'A member in business has a responsibility to further the legitimate aims of their employing organisation... [it is also necessary to] consider circumstances in which conflicts may be created with the duty to comply with the fundamental principles'.

5   **Refuse**. The request may have been made in ignorance and good faith, so you should attempt to explain the technical, legal and ethical principles that apply.

6   **Protects employees from suffering detriment for internal whistleblowing, or reporting to a regulator, in good faith**. The whistleblower should have reasonable grounds to believe that a criminal offence has been or will be committed, that the health or safety of any individual is likely to be endangered, that the environment has been, or is being damaged and/or that information on any of the above is being deliberately concealed. Public disclosure is a more complicated situation, requiring legal advice.

INDEX

Notes

Notes

REVIEW FORM

How have you used this Text?
(Tick one box only)

☐ Home study

☐ On a course_____

☐ Other _____

Why did you decide to purchase this Text?
(Tick one box only)

☐ Have used BPP Texts in the past

☐ Recommendation by friend/colleague

☐ Recommendation by a college lecturer

☐ Saw advertising

☐ Other _____

During the past six months do you recall seeing/receiving either of the following?
(Tick as many boxes as are relevant)

☐ Our advertisement in Accounting Technician

☐ Our Publishing Catalogue

Which (if any) aspects of our advertising do you think are useful?
(Tick as many boxes as are relevant)

☐ Prices and publication dates of new editions

☐ Information on Text content

☐ Details of our free online offering

☐ None of the above

Your ratings, comments and suggestions would be appreciated on the following areas of this Text.

	Very useful	Useful	Not useful
Introductory section	☐	☐	☐
Quality of explanations	☐	☐	☐
How it works	☐	☐	☐
Chapter tasks	☐	☐	☐
Chapter Overviews	☐	☐	☐
Test your learning	☐	☐	☐
Index	☐	☐	☐

	Excellent	Good	Adequate	Poor
Overall opinion of this Text	☐	☐	☐	☐

Do you intend to continue using BPP Products?   ☐ Yes   ☐ No

Please note any further comments and suggestions/errors on the reverse of this page. The author of this edition can be e-mailed at: suedexter@bpp.com

Please return to: Sue Dexter, Publishing Director, BPP Learning Media Ltd, FREEPOST, London, W12 8BR.

REVIEW FORM (continued)

TELL US WHAT YOU THINK

Please note any further comments and suggestions/errors below.